BRAND NAME KIDS

BRAND NAME KIDS

RICHARD PATTERSON, JR.

Power Books

Fleming H. Revell
Old Tappan, New Jersey

Scripture quotations identified NAS are from the New American Standard Bible, © The Lockman Foundation 1960, 1962, 1963, 1968, 1971, 1972, 1973, 1975, 1977.

Scripture quotations identified NIV are from the Holy Bible, New International Version, copyright © 1973, 1978, 1984 International Bible Society. Used by permission of Zondervan Bible Publishers.

Scripture quotations identified KJV are from the King James Version of the Bible.

LIBRARY OF CONGRESS
Library of Congress Cataloging-in-Publication Data

Patterson, Richard, 1948–
    Brand name kids / Richard Patterson, Jr.
        p. cm.
    Bibliography: p.
    ISBN 0-8007-5287-2
    1. Parenting—United States. 2. Parent and child—United States.
3. Parenting—Religious   aspects—Christianity.   4. Child   psychology—
United States. I. Title.
HQ755.8.P397 1988
305.2'3—dc19   88-18204
                                                                         CIP

Copyright © 1988 by Richard Patterson, Jr.
Published by the Fleming H. Revell Company
Old Tappan, New Jersey 07675
Printed in the United States of America

TO my parents,
Eugene and Gladys Patterson,
who gave their children
not only the special treasures of childhood,
but the inestimable gift
of a living faith.

Contents

Part II: The Hope

Preface

I n recent years both social observers and professionals who work with children have come to the startling conclusion that significant, somewhat disturbing changes in the nature of childhood have somehow taken place. We see the effects of these changes reflected in the lives and spirits of our children every day.

"Hurrying" or "hothousing" children, for example, or the disappearance or loss of childhood are all terms used to describe these changes. Though analyzed and evaluated from a variety of perspectives, there is general agreement on one fact—these changes threaten childhood and, therefore, children as we have come to understand them in the last century.

A casual observer might only say that children today seem so much more grown up than when he or she was a child. What they sense is true. Children *do* seem to grow up a lot faster these days; they *do* seem to "put away childish things" a lot sooner than their parents or grandparents.

In today's world there are at least *three* certainties: death, taxes, and change. Change is a fact of life and childhood has not been unaffected. But Christians who live in a close relationship with a living, loving, sovereign God, a God who cares deeply about children, need not be resigned to all change as inevitable and immutable. We can pray, hope, and work for change of our own.

The gradual diminishment of childhood has produced changes that have resulted in more than just social or emotional losses to children. There are real spiritual losses, also. Children are whole people, people whose mental, emotional, physical, and spiritual aspects are all part of a greater whole. Losses in one area affect the others in some way.

This book is an attempt to examine the loss of that long and protected period of nurture and dependency that has been such a treasure to children over the past century and a half. A holistic perspective will be used to examine the changes that have occurred, including an examination of the serious spiritual consequences of these changes for children. Because I had not seen such an examination of the changing nature of childhood from this perspective, I began this modest effort.

For over fifteen years I have worked professionally with children attempting to help nurture their faith. Over that time I have seen again and again how invaluable and of what inestimable worth to the spiritual life of adults is the innocent, dependent spirit of a child. It is a precious, irreplaceable gift that children offer adults. As childhood vanishes, this gift goes with it. Yet I am convinced and indeed hopeful that it need not and must not be so.

Acknowledgments

I want to thank those who have, in one way or another, made their own substantial contributions to this effort.

Mr. Clif Cartland, former editor and publisher of *Family Life Today*, is a champion of children and families. He was the first to invite me to write for publication. Directly from that opportunity and his encouragement came the invitation to write this book.

My dear friends and colleagues in ministry Wayne and Paula Glidden have been co-workers with me in the truest sense. Their encouragement, comments, patient typing and retyping, and editing (and improving!) my labored grammar made this effort possible. While I would not want them to bear any responsibility for this book's opinions or weaknesses (which may be largely identical), they certainly deserve a major share of any small amount of credit it may receive.

Lastly, my wife and two sons cheerfully put up with my regular absences from family times while I was writing. I am happy to thank them, also, for their indispensable permission and encouragement.

Introduction: For Adults Only

I could feel it coming, but it was still a shock to have to say it: "My twelve-year-old son is as tall as I am." I told a friend, "He is already borrowing my best shirts. My shoes are safe only because his feet are *already* bigger than mine!"

Those many hormones raging through his adolescent body produced undeniable physical evidence. His childhood was just about over. Physically, he was already the size of an adult.

Was he an adult? That hardly seemed the case. Whatever distinguishes an adult from a child has to be more than just physical size. It has to do even more with the processes of thinking and choosing.

We adults live with one eye on the present, the "now," and one on the future. We can think rationally about our situations and decide to postpone actions, acquisitions, and commitments until the "right time." Sometimes, in making those decisions, we know instinctively that the "right time" is indefinite and perhaps may never come.

In sharp contrast, young children live marvelously and totally in the world of "now." My younger son, at six, struggled to understand a future just a few days ahead. He was not at all interested in giving up one ice-cream cone today for the promise of three next week. He wasn't sure when next week was, anyway!

Not only are we adults supposed to be able to delay the gratification of our immediate desires in favor of a higher goal, we're supposed to be self-disciplined and able to exercise self-restraint. Meanwhile, our young children struggle to control the impulse to "punch first, ask questions later," when they think a playmate has broken one of their toys.

Self-restraint, concern for the future, and a capacity for delayed gratification—these are distinguishing characteristics of adults.[1] Yet by this definition, adults seem increasingly to be in short supply today.

I confess to being basically impatient. I hate to wait! I'll never forget standing in one of those seemingly endless "queues" in a British store some years ago. I thought, *This could never happen in America. We simply wouldn't stand for it. We'd all go to K-Mart, where, whenever there are at least three people in each checkout line, they open a new one!* We Americans hate to wait for the satisfaction of any immediate desire.

"The future is now," and, "you can have it all," are more than just clever advertising slogans. They have captured the spirit of our time. Microwaves, fast food, and young couples struggling under oppressive mortgage payments testify eloquently to our inability to wait for anything or to trust in the future.

Perhaps that is part of the secret appeal of children and childhood. Children know nothing of the fear of the future. They truly do live for today. They "say the darndest things" with little restraint, and somehow it sounds cute! They can "stop and smell the roses" anytime they wish.

Perhaps that's why so many adults today seem to wish they could still act like children. That wish was illustrated very poignantly by Jake Buggs, one of the characters in the hit film, *She's Having a Baby*, starring the popular young actors Kevin Bacon and Elizabeth McGovern.

Jake has just graduated from college and is soon to be married. Sitting in his car with his best friend, he confesses that he is afraid. He's not afraid of his wife-to-be at all. But he does fear taking on the adult responsibilities of marriage. In a moving moment, we hear him reflect sadly that his youth has gone too quickly. "I still want to be a child," he says. But he knows it's too late.

What did Jake mean, exactly, when he said he still wanted to be a child? "I don't want to accept the responsibility of making and keeping a lifelong marriage commitment. Who knows what might happen?" "I don't want to have to be sexually self-disciplined. Why should I miss out on the fun? I still want to do what I want to do when I want to do it without worrying about next year or even next week." "I'm certainly not ready to consider postponing or sacrificing any personal economic or career goals for the sake of the children."

Jake might have meant any or all those things, and he might have been speaking on behalf of many adults today. "I still want to be a child. What's the matter with that?"

The "matter" of course is that children need *adults*, in order to be children and grow through childhood into adults themselves. By giving children the gift of a stable marriage, a period of protection, nurture, and dependency, by making the necessary sacrifices for their children's future, and by *being* adults themselves, adults make childhood, that period of growing up into adulthood, possible for children.

These kinds of adults, however, are far less numerous than at any time in the past thirty years. As a result, childhood is in danger.

In the first seven chapters that follow, I attempt to show how and why this is so and what some of the implications are for the future of our children and our society. In most cases, I try to offer some suggestions as to how concerned and caring adults can act to preserve the benefits of childhood for the future.

We'll be traveling over some rough terrain during this journey. We'll take a hard look at some real problems and challenges facing children as they try to grow up today.

But the picture really isn't as dark as it may seem at first glance. The final two chapters focus on many of the reasons for a sturdy hope in the future of childhood. In those chapters, we'll meet some real "pioneers," folks who are relearning and rediscovering creative and exciting ways of parenting children today.

These people whom we'll meet are "regular folks," just like

you and me. What they have learned comes as a result of a lot of trying. They had some success and some failure. But they've learned some important things that they're happy to share.

As we meet them, we'll discover that even though children *do* face some serious problems in growing up today, there are new, helpful attitudes beginning to emerge among adults.

For example, surveys show that what parents want most for their children is not achievement or success but personal happiness and satisfaction.[2] Men and women are discovering all over again the deep satisfaction gained from parenting—sacrifices and all. Having tried "being children" for a while, some adults are deeply dissatisfied with it. They've discovered again the old spiritual truth that self-fulfillment is found, not in self, but in giving love to others, even children!

That's not to say that struggles and tensions have all disappeared. We'll survey some of the attitudes toward work that force men and women into the false choice of *"either* my career *or* caring for my children."* We'll also see some of the creative ways working parents have begun to resolve those tensions.

We'll meet some couples who have refused to choose *either* career *or* caring for children and have instead sought to work out a happy blending of both career and care for children.[3] The product is a whole new integrated concept of "career," which includes both.

For men, this new concept of career means truly "growing up" and reclaiming the joys, privileges, and responsibilities of being full coparents of their children. For women, it may mean discovering new models (or rediscovering old ones, as we'll see) of working and caring. Putting down the two-ton briefcase[4] can be a moment of exhilarating freedom!

There are other hopeful signs we will explore, also. There are indications that adults may be discovering a new appreciation for those previously distasteful adult characteristics: self-restraint, capacity for delayed gratification, and concern for the future. We trace these indications in the final chapter.

Not the least of these hopeful signs is the indication that the "baby boomers" are returning to church. This whole generation of current and soon-to-be parents are beginning to attend church once again, and they are bringing their children with them.

This "lost generation" of parents is returning to the institutional church, it seems, motivated by a desire to provide their children with "good values."[5] Certainly, the church can provide those. How wonderful it would be if they, and their children, found the living Lord Jesus Christ there, also!

I hope it will be clear that many of the observations and suggestions offered here are directed to people who have the freedom to choose to act on them. I recognize that there may be single parents (mostly mothers) reading this who simply have no choice but to work, support their families, and put their children in whatever care situation they can manage.

I know that, even in some dual-career families, both spouses cannot really choose *not* to work full-time outside the home. About 70 percent of working mothers are married to husbands who make less than $20,000 annually.[6] Do these women have a "choice"? Perhaps, but which of us would choose differently?

These women, poor women, single mothers, mothers struggling to help the family survive economically (not just enjoy the "extras") deserve no "guilt trips" from me or anyone else. They already sacrifice more for their children day after day than they ever thought they could. They are nothing less than heroes. Their children will one day rise up and call them blessed.[7]

Other parents, however, have much more freedom to choose. It is to them that the observations which follow are directed.

There is probably very little that is original in these chapters. If the reader observes more attention paid to identifying problems than suggesting correctives, I will not argue. Nonetheless, what I attempt to offer to all parents and concerned adults is a distinctly Christian perspective on this situation, something not apparently available to date. New, alternative, and practical ways of protecting the benefits of childhood for future generations are offered.

In spite of the very real difficulties children face, there are adults around who are adults in the truest sense. They understand that "children are the living messages we send to a time we will not see."[8] Those who are Christians realize that the meaning they send through their children will live on for an eternal future.

These truest of adults see their children as precious gifts from God, worthy of their best efforts. So they gladly pour themselves out for their children as their heavenly parent has done for them.

Self-restraint and self-sacrifice are no problem to these parents. They are quite willing to go slower up the career ladder (or to refrain from climbing it at all), if necessary, and to do what it takes to make their marriages work!

Their goal is simple. They want to send this message to the future: "Our children *are* our greatest blessing, and we pass them on to you, confident that they will bless others, also." These are the kind of adults children need today. It is with the hope of encouraging them, even just a little, that these words are written.

BRAND NAME KIDS

Part I

THE LOSSES

ONE

The Loss
of Childhood

He is awakened abruptly at 6:00 A.M. Rubbing the sleep from his eyes, he gets dressed, eats his breakfast, and is ready to leave the house before 7:00. The carpool will be by soon and he will be "at work" by 7:30.

It will be a long day before he finally arrives home, dead tired at 5:00 P.M. That's earlier than some of his friends get home, but then he's only four years old! Both Mom and Dad work so he spends his day at a nearby day-care center. The people there are nice enough, but someday he'd just like to play with his own toys in his own house with his own mom or dad nearby!

Across town in the projects a nine-year-old girl helps her mom get the three younger children ready for school. School wouldn't be such a bad place to be all day if only it wasn't so hard! She tries to ignore them when the other kids call her "dummy" or "retard," but it sure does hurt. There never seems to be enough time or energy left after dinner to work hard at her homework.

When school is over that day, she takes her time walking home. Why hurry? It's no fun spending all your time helping Mom look after the children and helping with dinner and chores. But Mom's all alone and she works hard too. It sure would be nice to be alone and play with her doll for a while or skip rope outside with the other girls!

These two children are different in many ways. They live in different parts of town and have different types of families and economic circumstances. But they do have one thing in common with each other and with millions of other children across the country: They are children losing their childhood.

For children, childhood is nothing less than a treasure. It is an all too brief time of carefree innocence and unquestioning trust in life. Childhood is a humane and gentle gift to children of a time and a space within which to grow and learn to live, guided and protected by loving adults.

Childhood is a treasure that comes enclosed in a sturdy chest made of the commitment to a lasting marriage. The hinges on the chest close tight, sealing out for a time the problems and burdens of being grown up. Safely inside remain the precious jewels of a trusting, dependent heart, a hopeful, loving spirit, and a spontaneous faith in God.

But for the little boy of four whose daily schedule could easily be mistaken for his father's, or the nine-year-old girl who carries a heavy load both at home and at school, childhood is a vanishing treasure.

To be sure, being a child has never been easy anywhere, at any time, and to assume otherwise is to be unnecessarily romantic. In the England of Dickens's *Oliver Twist*, young children earned their keep from Fagin-like characters who used them to steal. Others were mutilated to make them more appealing beggars. Conditions in orphanages often approached slavery.

Only a generation or two ago it was common for young children to do the chores on the family farm or work in the family shop before and after school. Parents died in those days, too, leaving behind a "single" parent.

The job of growing up, learning to make sense of life, learning how to get along with others, learning to speak properly and to read and to master a growing, changing body would be hard enough for most children without any added difficulties!

For the last century, however, young children have had a special ally in their struggle to be grown up, to be physically, emotionally, and spiritually mature. This special ally has been that twelve- to seventeen-year period of protection and nurture by adults that came to be known as childhood.

My wife and I are the parents of two boys. Whenever folks ask us if we miss not having a girl, we quickly assure them that we are very content! Boys are much easier to raise than girls, we tell them. How can you "miss" the constant hassles in many families over the question of when a preteen daughter can wear eye shadow (and how much!)? Would we miss trying to decide at what age that strapless dress would be appropriate?

These questions and the heated family discussions they occasion are relatively new in history, however, because childhood itself is a recent phenomenon. Before the modern understanding of childhood began to develop, probably in the sixteenth century, there were only two periods of life, infancy and adulthood. [1]

In the Middle Ages, for example, by the time a child was out of swaddling clothes he or she was dressed like any adult of that social class. The main feature distinguishing the child's clothes from that of the parents was the size. [2] By age seven, for all practical purposes, he or she was considered a miniature adult. Whatever brief childhood he or she enjoyed likely ended then. By seven, after mastering command of language, boys were apprenticed to a craftsman and joined in most aspects of adult life. [3]

Though the notion of childhood itself may be relatively new, its roots are ancient indeed. The Judeo-Christian tradition fostered the growing recognition in the last two centuries of the special status and needs of children that are at the heart of childhood.

How would Jesus treat children? There are no extensive biblical accounts of Jesus interacting with children, but there are some indications of His attitude. He welcomed children to come to Him, even when His disciples thought He was too busy or too important to be bothered with them. Obviously, that was not His attitude. [4]

Jesus probably played with children whenever He could, throwing them up in the air as they screamed with delight, tickling and hugging them. He not only loved children, He enjoyed and understood them: He made them, in their innocence and trusting dependence, models of faith for every adult.[5]

"Today, the yuppies only care about buying their first convertible," said Lee Iacocca, chairman of Chrysler Corporation. "They say 'We've got careers. We've got to wait until we're very much older to marry!' If that's the attitude, they'll never marry. They'll never have kids."[6]

What a far cry this attitude is from the biblical understanding of children as "a gift of the Lord" and His reward to His faithful people.[7] Surely children *are* more than the result of a sexual encounter and to be valued far beyond convertibles or other status symbols. But, as Iacocca's words reveal, this view of the unique value of children is under attack today, and that attack represents a serious threat to childhood.

Culture, Commitments, and Change

My wife's grandmother was proud of her family tree. Given the slightest reason, she would begin a proud recitation of all the people of accomplishment from whom she was descended. When she had finished, my wife would inevitably ask, in a teasing tone, "But Granny, what about all the horse thieves and philanderers?" That always ended the conversation quickly! Grandmother considered neither adultery nor divorce fit subjects for public discussion, especially if they involved one's own family!

Today Grandmother's attitude seems slightly quaint and naive. Newspapers and magazines are filled with public discussions and speculation about the latest divorce or affair of someone of notoriety.

The change in what was considered a fit topic of public discussion points to one of the most significant, and perhaps the most serious, losses that children have suffered today: the loss of the commitment to a lasting marriage. The loss of that commitment may carry away with it the loss of a commitment to a stable, nurturing family life for children, also.

The changes in our society that resulted in a loss of commitment to lasting marriage and stable family life began to accelerate rapidly after World War II. As Alvin Toffler characterized it, the past forty years have been a time of "future shock." During this period a new culture, a new constellation of moral and social values, finished the process of superimposing itself on an older one.[8]

This old culture could be characterized by its commitments. One such major commitment was a broad-based consensus on the value of marriage itself and marriages that lasted. "Open marriages," which permitted spouses to engage in extramarital sex, were not recognized as worthy of the name marriage. The current fascination with serial monogamy, a series of short-lived marriages, one after the other, would have been scandalous to my grandparents!

Nevertheless, the current high divorce rate did not simply spring full blown into American society in the past decade. Christopher Lasch, in his perceptive study of the family, *Haven in a Heartless World*, notes that the divorce rate increased fifteenfold between 1870 and 1920.[9] The forces undermining the commitment to lasting marriages and stable family life, so vital to children, have been at work for well over a century.

The change that has taken place in the last generation is one of attitude and acceptance. My wife's grandmother did not want to discuss the fact that anyone in her family might be divorced. As with a mentally ill relative or an alcoholic, a divorced person early in the century was the black sheep of the family. Divorce represented failure and loss. It was an embarrassment.

Anyone who followed national politics in the 1960s knows how true this was for Nelson Rockefeller. A multimillionaire and successful governor of New York, he tried repeatedly and unsuccessfully to capture the Republican nomination for President. Rockefeller was a popular governor of what was then the largest state in the nation. He had plenty of money to spend on his campaign for the nomination. But all his success as governor and all his money could not overcome one large handicap: He had divorced the mother of his children and married a younger woman.

Many political analysts of the time felt that Rockefeller's divorce was the major factor in thwarting his bid for the White House. The nation could not accept his divorce; social values of the time still supported the stability of marriage and discouraged divorce.

American couples in the early and mid-twentieth century dated, married, and had children in a culture that endorsed and supported lasting marriages and raising children. Whether driving in their Ramblers on a date and listening to the radio or listening to the jukebox at the soda shop, they heard songs that told of couples who were getting married because, after all, love and marriage were synonymous. Today the same radios and jukeboxes play songs where the boy or girl pleads with the other to spend the night.

At least as late as the mid-1960s, both the nation's religious institutions and its legal system supported the commitment to a lasting marriage, based both on biblical values and on more pragmatic ones. It was recognized that divorce caused an abundance of pain, especially for children. The state had an interest in promoting and protecting marital stability.

Most major religious denominations recognized a biblical mandate to uphold marriage. After all, did not the marriage ceremony quote Jesus saying, "What God hath joined together let not man put asunder"?[10] Divorced persons often were cut off from the sacraments and refused remarriage by their church as a way of discouraging divorce.

Divorce was as difficult legally as it was socially. In most states adultery (following a strict biblical interpretation) and perhaps desertion or cruelty were the only permissible grounds for divorce. In 1969 California became the first state to permit divorce on grounds of "irreconcilable differences," which was generally much easier to prove. Not until the recent advent of no-fault divorce, however, could the dissolution of a marriage be accomplished relatively easily.

If marriage commitments were supported by social values and institutions of the time, so was the commitment to having and raising children. Who can imagine "The Ozzie and Harriet Show" without David and Ricky? Who can picture Robert Young's success as "Husband [not Father] Knows Best"? Divorce happened, of course, but marriages were still expected to last and to produce children.

Children, as parents know, imply sacrifice. But if Americans were committed to anything, they were committed to their children and to just about any sacrifice their children's welfare required.

My wife graduated from high school in the early 1960s and almost did not go to college. Her parents, like many at that time, had to struggle economically to raise their five children, three girls and two boys. An education for the boys seemed the necessary choice in the face of economic realities.

But the decision was made that somehow all five would go to college. My wife was the oldest. As her high school career drew to a close, her mother went back to work. The extra income, together with a lot of scrimping, saving, and borrowing, made the dream a reality. All five children went to college.

This story is notable mainly for being so commonplace at the time. Having children implied a commitment to sacrifice for them so they "could have a better life than we did," so they could go to college and "be somebody." It was taken for granted.

Immigrant parents worked long hours at sometimes two tedious jobs so their children could go to college. Marriage partners stayed together and were more likely to work at staying together. They fulfilled their marriage commitments, sometimes in spite of a death of love or intimacy "for the good of the children."

Great sacrifices were made by women who postponed or abandoned careers to care for their young children full time, as my own mother did. They believed the social workers and other professionals who preached the virtues of domesticity and portrayed the good mother as the one who stayed home to care for the needs of her young children.[11] These parents made commitments to each other and to their children; they were prepared to sacrifice to keep those commitments.

In the last decade, however, such commitments have been superseded by a new, overarching commitment: the commitment to *me* and my personal fulfillment. Childrearing, with all the sacrifice it requires, is often seen by couples today as a major obstacle to that self-fulfillment. To some women, children are seen as preventing them from "taking their rightful place in the world of work."[12] Children, it seems, offer so little in the way of fulfillment today that, as one magazine reported, they are now running behind automobiles as items of consumer preference![13]

Sociologist Robert Bellah in his book *Habits of the Heart: Individualism and Commitment in America* recounts a telling discussion with a man identified only as Brian.[14] Brian, a highly successful businessperson, was driven by his commitment to success and gave everything to his job and company. He neglected his marriage. After fifteen years of neglect, his wife divorced him.

The divorce proved to be a traumatic event that forced Brian to evaluate his priorities. He remarried and later told Bellah how he and his second wife have "discovered a new sense of energy and mutual devotion and commitment sufficient to make family life a joy."[15]

When pressed to explain the reasons behind such a radical change in his commitments and behavior, Bellah says Brian's answers boil down to a shift in his notion of what would make him happy. "His new goal—devotion to marriage and children—seems as arbitrary and unexamined as his earlier pursuit of material success."[16]

That is the essence of interpersonal commitments today: arbitrary and unexamined. They are no longer constrained by the biblical values of permanence and covenant (an unconditional, unbreakable self-giving) but instead are based on "what works for me." Tragically, for children and childhood, commitments to marriage and children today are often built on the same shifting sands.

Children, Families, and Heroes

American culture in this century has come to idolize the individual who, free of commitments to spouse and children, goes about doing whatever seems right. This self-reliant, self-sufficient individual needs no one and nothing more than the freedom to do his or her "thing," whatever it may turn out to be. Here is the new all-American hero.

Despite the fact that we Americans live in a highly interdependent society, the myth of this unentangled individual lives on, smiling down from countless billboards along every highway, sitting alone around a campfire contentedly smoking a cigarette. However impractical in reality or unhealthy emotionally, the freedom to do my own thing unencumbered by commitments to others has become, in recent years, a cherished American goal. To the extent that such individualism is cherished and pursued, it cannot help but weaken our willingness to make and keep lasting marriage commitments and sacrifice for our children.

Our American heroes are idolized and envied precisely because they are "free" of families and therefore, it is implied "really free." They are the Dirty Harrys, Rambos, and Kojaks. This worship of the lone individual, free of family ties, who rights the wrongs of society points to an antifamily strain in American cultural values.

In a strong and healthy society how shallow a view of heroes this is: the real heroes are the men and women who ". . . hold the world together one home at a time: the parents and grandparents who forego pleasures, delay purchases, foreclose options, and commit most of their lives to the noblest of undertakings of citizenship: raising children who, resting on the shoulders of the previous generation, will see farther than we and reach higher."[17]

A popular comic strip jokingly depicted a home delivery service for condoms so a newly acquainted couple could take precautions against AIDS and still have a sexual relationship.

Not only has the moral consensus that upheld the commitment to marriage declined, but technology has eased the process!

Modern technology, which has created the birth control pill, vasectomies, and "safe abortions," has also created a new classification of sexual relationship: recreational sex. In the past thirty years the development of highly effective, relatively convenient, and inexpensive contraceptives has for the first time made possible the separation of sex from the context of marriage and children.[18]

Modern technology feeds off these desires by inventing ways to help get things done the way people want them and to get them done as conveniently as possible. The virtual explosion of abortions in the past fifteen years is a graphic illustration of how unborn children can be seen as "inconvenient" and then efficiently eliminated. The union of individualism and technology unrestrained by values affirming marriage and children has taken a terrible toll on children and childhood today.

Why do people have children anyway? A century ago, when it was much more difficult *not* to have children, children were more often valued as a gift from the Lord. One's children were in turn one's gift to the future, the repository of one's dreams, values, and life's work.

Studies today show that couples now see far fewer advantages to having children than they did in the first half of this century. When they think about having children, they think mainly of the disadvantages: the high cost of raising children, the disruptions to their life style, and the sacrifices required of self and career.[19] What has emerged is a new understanding of children and childhood as disposable, debatable, and, most tragically, expendable.

The Loss of Innocence

In late 1986 Surgeon General C. Everett Koop created a firestorm of controversy by suggesting that sex education aimed at preventing the spread of AIDS be started in third grade (which for some children is as young as seven years old). Children, he said, needed to be instructed in the importance of using protection in the face of this epidemic. His most virulent detractors accused him of advocating "safe sodomy" for third graders, while other observers simply felt that children's young minds wouldn't make sense of this information.

Alerting (perhaps, some would say, alarming) young children to the dangers of sexual activity is an example of the loss of innocence of children today. The childhood that adults put away as they grew up (but nostalgically remember all their lives) is that period of carefree innocence when life was not yet weighed down by the adult burdens of sex, power, and aggression.

In the past adults labored to protect and prolong childhood innocence. Soon enough, children would have to face the struggles and frustrations, the cynicism and pessimism of much of adult life. Today, as author Marie Winn puts it, "this age of protection" of a child's innocence has given way to an "age of preparation" for adult life.[20] Life is tough and getting ahead in this highly complex and rapidly changing society requires getting a head start early in life and pushing hard to keep ahead of the pack.

"Getting ahead" often means that nursery school children are taught to use a computer and elementary school students no longer have recess, that morning and afternoon break from the classroom, to go outside for unstructured play. Instead of a time of carefree innocence and play, childhood is becoming a stressful time.

Play is an important "stress valve" for children as well as adults, but unstructured play time is fast becoming an unafford-able luxury for young children.[21] Ignored is the fact that unstructured play is serious business for a child. It not only relieves stress, but is often how the child works out problems in his or her relationships.[22]

"Getting ahead" means that reading is now taught in many kindergartens, despite evidence that many children are not developmentally ready to read before six years old. The loss of play time and the stress of having to learn to read at an early age mean that early childhood school days have lost much of their relaxed, playful atmosphere and have become much more achievement oriented and stressful. In other words, they have become more adult.

There is certainly nothing relaxed and carefree about the millions of eight- and nine-year-old children who come home to an empty house after school each day. Taught to be suspicious of strangers at the door, cautious in answering the phone, and worried at every unexplained noise they hear, these latch-key children carry a heavy burden.

They have been assigned the responsibility of "self-care," in reality a term for "no care" and lack of adequate adult supervision. Sometimes the burden of self-care is compounded by the responsibility for younger siblings after school until a parent arrives home. In previous generations these responsibilities were assumed to belong properly to adults, not children. Certainly children have always had to help look after younger siblings, but there was always a competent adult nearby who was responsible.

Some years ago a good friend of mine died suddenly in his early forties, leaving behind his wife and three young children. The oldest child, a daughter, was then about twelve years old. Because she was the oldest, her mother turned to her in those early grief-stricken months for advice on family finances, discipline of her toddler brother, and the prospects of dating again.

For many spouses, especially those "robbed" of the emotional intimacy and support of a partner by divorce, a child becomes a surrogate spouse. He or she is called upon to think and act in more adult ways than his or her natural emotional development at that time would allow. Questions about the family's financial survival, parental dating, and similar topics impose on young children the real stress of having to confront issues and make decisions clearly beyond their scope.

My youngest son, who is seven, goes through a predictable routine every night after he receives his good-night kiss. "Where will you be, Daddy? Where will Mommy be? Where will my brother be?" Before he can relax and go to sleep he needs to know that the people he loves and who take care of him will be nearby as he sleeps.

One of a young child's greatest fears is the fear of abandonment, especially by the parents on whom he or she is so clearly and deeply dependent. Abandonment is literally terrifying, and even a short separation in a church nursery or at home with a babysitter may be traumatizing.

The painful separation and abandonment of divorce creates in a child a terrible sense of pain and loss, vulnerability, and an "internal chaos" not quickly calmed. "I am weak and vulnerable. Who will care for me now? Will *anyone* care for me? Am I still loved? Is this just a temporary separation like one of Dad's business trips? I sure hope so."

The results of a ten-year study of children involved in divorce underline the emotional trauma involved. The experience of a family breakup can so disturb a child that he or she may become psychologically unable to live a happy adult life.[23] Such children have academic problems also. They are absent from school more frequently, more likely to repeat a grade, and have a lower I.Q.[24]

When forty-nine states passed a no-fault divorce law, no one understood the radically debilitating effect no-fault divorce would have on family stability and the emotional and spiritual health of children. Children of divorce are not only more prone to unhappiness, psychological referral, and academic problems, but their faith is also affected. When your parents have split up and your safe and secure world has been shattered, it is a lot more difficult to trust in a God who is said to always be there for you, always caring for you. Isn't that what Mom and Dad were supposed to do?

Children and Poverty

The loss of commitment to marriage has plunged many children and their parents (usually single mothers) into poverty.

Newsweek magazine pointed to "the skyrocketing rise in the number of single parent families," many headed by teens, as "the one cultural phenomenon that ensnares families into poverty more than any other."[25]

Today, one in five families with young children is headed by a single parent; about half of those are below the poverty level.[26] A study of California's no-fault divorce law showed that the effect of the average divorce was to decrease the standard of living of the woman and her minor children by 73 percent while *increasing* the male's by 43 percent.[27]

Poverty can make life rough for young children right from the start. Lack of proper nutrition often affects their developing minds. They tend to do less well in school, drop out more frequently, and have a harder time getting a good job when they get older.[28] They usually get substandard health care, also.

Tragically, the number of children in poverty is especially high among blacks. These children begin life handicapped by the double whammy of poverty and the lingering effects of racism. Their young, still-developing bodies, minds, and spirits are being crippled and crushed daily by the effects of poverty.

Harvard psychologist Alvin Poussaint, consultant to the popular TV series "The Cosby Show," says children living in poverty suffer emotionally, also. Early in life they feel the sharp pain of failure, self-doubt, and helpless frustration that accompanies poverty.[29]

A child can easily feel "no good" when everyone else seems to have so much that she cannot have. Something must be wrong with you when you do not see any hope that can change your situation. It hurts. It hurts a lot.

These children learn quickly in life to have no dreams, no hope. Dreams only disappoint. Hope only leads to hopelessness. Many of these children represent what one social worker called "a large group of unhealthy, illiterate, non-functional youth" who are likely to become a "non-functional work-force."[30]

They are already well along the way to becoming a permanent "underclass" that our society will not want to acknowledge and our churches will not understand how to reach. Their plight requires more than I have to offer in this or even in another book devoted entirely to them. But a book is not really the answer, anyway. We can all see their problem already. The question is when we will choose to do something about it.

Poverty is one (but only one) of the great cripplers of a child's self-esteem. Self-esteem, which develops (or not) during childhood, is that healthy sense of value one puts on oneself; the understanding that "I am somebody," important in my own right. It is an understanding that one's life is a precious gift from a loving God.

In turn, self-esteem is the childhood foundation on which adult emotional and spiritual health is built. This foundation is being seriously weakened in the lives of many children, black and white, today.

Television and the Family

Even in those "intact" families today, there is often something missing. "Family time" together has been lost to the television. Families eat together less, and when they do, they often do so while watching the television. Families spend less and less time together overall.

What do children lose as a result? They lose the opportunity to experience the development of a sense of family unity and communication as they talk to each other over a meal and catch up with each other's lives. They lose a sense of belonging to a "family" that spends time together because they really care for each other. They lose the emotional intimacy and affirmation such experiences provide.

Building that kind of healthy family takes time and effort. It takes commitment, and often it seems to take more than tired, hassled two-career families have to give. But children, like adults, have to find a sense of belonging somewhere. They have to feel affirmed by emotional intimacy from someone—if not their family, then peers and premature sexual relationships.

Television plays a central role in the loss of childhood innocence. Afternoon soap operas and evening prime time series are full of explosive, seemingly uncontrollable adult passions and violence. The evening news provides young children a vivid picture of most adult weaknesses and failures. In such a world as television portrays, a world where adult violence is rampant, where children die of AIDS, and the President is called a liar almost daily, who can blame a child for becoming anxious or cynical? Who can be surprised if a young child quickly loses trust in the ability of adults to "take care of things"?

The Tyranny of the Family

"How to Be a Better (Working) Mother" read the headline in a woman's magazine. Begin by giving up your guilt, the article advised, guilt over not being with your young child most of the time while he or she is growing up, and guilt over depriving your child of a "golden childhood." No mother owes her child an idyllic youth, the author assures us, and probably couldn't provide one anyway![31]

These, and countless articles like them, are published frequently and read by working mothers every month. They point to a real dilemma. The heated debate is carried on everywhere from magazines to church Bible studies: the pros and cons of working mothers (a better debate might be over working spouses of either sex).

For Christians concerned with the welfare of young children, the debate is a painful clash of competing values. On one side is the call for economic self-sufficiency for women and on the other is the fear that realization of that self-sufficiency "would undermine equally important values associated with the family."[32]

One of those values so central to childhood is the notion of the prolonged dependency of young children, lasting at least into early adolescence. In the past this dependence on parents gave young children time to grow up slowly and carefully, always guided and protected by parents. Dependence diminished gradually over time until, at seventeen or eighteen years of age, the child took major responsibility for his or her own life.

Today, however, this childhood dependence is under attack. Militant feminists call for its shortening as the only way to break "the tyranny of the biological family" over women.[33] It seems they feel that only when we return to the medieval order where a child of five or six no longer requires the full-time care of his or her mother can women begin to have the freedom to achieve economic and personal fulfillment.

This is a painful situation for women, their families, and their children, who are caught right in the middle of it all. Until the debate is resolved (hopefully, on the side of the needs of young children), children will continue to lose the dependency and family stability so essential to their healthy development.

But there are some hopeful signs for children. The divorce rate has leveled off in recent years and begun to decline. Whatever the "me generation" does, polls say that a good family life is its number one social value, even above physical health, personal fulfillment, or individual freedom of choice.[34]

Government has recognized the serious losses sustained by children and the family in recent decades and is attempting to reconstruct social supports for family life. The White House Conference on Families in 1979 and the Reports of the Attorney General's Commission of Pornography and the White House Working Group on the Family, both issued in 1986, are hopeful signs.

Governmental policies cannot "save" childhood. They can, however, lead public opinion, shape public values, and influence the direction of our culture in a way that supports children and their families.

Government has much at stake in rescuing childhood. It is during childhood, in the context of family life, that children learn to make and keep commitments to others, to respect and obey authority, and to seek common goals with others. No democratic nation can survive long without these values. Within the scope of its limited sphere, then, we must ask our government to begin the task of reconstructing public support for childhood and family life.

"Onward, Christian soldiers! Marching as to war" goes the old hymn. Children and their families need the church to march to war again on behalf of children and childhood. Americans have always been a nation of churchgoers. Our values are both democratic and biblical. To children and families struggling with the lure of personal self-fulfillment against older values of family stability and self-sacrifice, the Christian church can offer support, encouragement, and hope to "make it all worth it."

Jesus said, "Let the little children come to me, and do not hinder them, for the kingdom of heaven belongs to such as these."[35] As the treasure of childhood vanishes from among us, we all, children and adults alike, are the losers. Children lose trust in adults. They can't depend on adult care anymore. And this childlike trust and dependency, Jesus said, is what makes their faith the model for us adults.

As our children lose the ability to trust us, they lose the ability to trust in God, their Father. As they lose the ability to feel loved and secure in their families, they lose the ability to feel loved by God and the Christian family, the church. They lose the spiritual and moral foundations on which a truly happy life is built, and we lose a little bit more of "the kingdom of heaven" among us.

TWO

The Loss
of Innocence

I n a small room in the National Gallery of Art in Washington, D.C., hang four paintings by the nineteenth century artist Thomas Cole. Each painting is entitled *The Voyage of Life* and each is an allegorical representation of life's four stages, childhood, adulthood, old age, and death.

Cole's painting of childhood depicts a cherubic child reclining on a bed of flowers and riding in a boat. The boat, steered by an angel, appears to be gliding peacefully along a river. This painting reflects the prevailing understanding of childhood in nineteenth- and early twentieth-century America: a time of innocence, a relaxed carefree period of life protected by divine authority itself.

In America today, the loss of childhood innocence is widely prevalent. Innocence, as Cole painted it, is that quality of children that springs from the absence of the need to carry responsibilities more appropriate for adults. Childhood innocence is built on the foundation of the child's "right" to play freely and spontaneously, to be naively optimistic about life, to be free of adult cares and worries, and to be guided and protected by caring adults.

This innocence is not some romantic, charming quality that nostalgic adults, grown older and more cynical, wistfully attribute to children. Rather, it is a real and essential part of the treasure of childhood bestowed on children in the last century and a half.

One major reason for the loss of childhood innocence is the

disappearance of play. The propensity of children "to engage in that extraordinary series of behaviors characterized as 'play' is perhaps the single great dividing line" between the world of children and that of adults.[1] An adult works; a child plays. Almost by itself, playing defines children.

Play is the stuff of life for young children. A few weeks of regular observation at a local preschool demonstrated to me how serious a child's play can be. Having visited the school once a week over a period of months, I observed the children enrolled there and saw how they coped with the various problems and stresses in their lives. One day I watched a boy and girl, each about four years old, playing house. They had a doll, representing their baby, and they were arguing over it. It was clearly a girl doll, which pleased the little girl. But the young boy insisted they find a boy doll for their baby; he did not want a girl baby.

The children's teacher understood the drama presented here. The boy's mother had just brought home a baby sister and he was experiencing the all too common feelings of being "displaced" by his new sister in the attention and affection of his parents. Maybe, he must have thought, it would be different with a baby brother.

Another child was pretending to be a super hero. With a towel for a cape he was ready to jump off a table that had become, through the magic of imagination, a frighteningly high building. Unhurt and smiling after his twelve-inch-high jump, the child felt quite super and competent indeed. This feeling was in sharp contrast, no doubt, to what a four year old feels most of the time in a world where he or she is usually uncomfortably dependent on adults.

What good is play to a young child? As became clear to me, play is a window into the mind and heart of a young child. Play reveals how he or she understands the world, the problems it presents, and how he or she would like it to be.[2]

For the young boy at the preschool who wanted a baby brother instead of a sister, his play was his way of expressing frustration (he could not articulate it) and then coping with it. For the boy playing super hero, it was his way of feeling competent and building his sense of self-esteem. For all children it is a way of experiencing the sheer pleasure of having fun.

Play is an essential part of childhood. It is a time of "free exploration and experimentation," a time when young children at play learn "about each other and about how to handle themselves as people." Childhood is the time when, through play, children learn to put together their sense of themselves and their world. It is the one time they are still able to play and to dream.[3]

"Why don't you do something besides watch television?" we parents are prone to say to our children, or "Be creative once in a while." But "being creative" with one's leisure time does not just happen. It requires two things that are in short supply among many children today: leisure time and adults who tolerate and even encourage their children to enjoy it.

Time to play spontaneously and creatively is being squeezed out of the lives of young children today. Many preschools and kindergartens, for example, have shifted the focus of their curriculum away from an emphasis on social and emotional development (which is fostered by interactive playtime) and toward a concentration on academic skills development.

Beginning reading and simple computer operations are now being taught to preschool and kindergarten children. Some preschools and kindergartens assign homework; some give achievement tests to monitor the children's progress and track their readiness for first grade. One elite private school near our home requires a comprehensive evaluation and recommendation from a child's nursery school teacher as a prerequisite for admission to its kindergarten.

This increase in time spent on developing academic skills has produced a corresponding decrease: Much less time is spent on spontaneous free play (the kind I observed at the preschool).

But will not this help give young children the head start they need in this complex, everchanging world? Probably not; it may even slow them down. Research has shown that play helps preschoolers develop areas of their psychological functioning that are basic to learning how to read and to overall knowledge development. Playtime is exactly what they need *at that stage of their psychological and emotional development* to be able to achieve later academic success.[4]

We parents are so proud of our young children when they first learn to read; any difficulty in learning to read raises fears of our child being slow or learning disabled. But if the child is under the age of six (and especially if it is a boy), he may not be physically ready to read. Reading requires that a child possess a complicated set of language and other skills; some children under six simply have not undergone the physical development necessary for these skills to grow. They will come, but not yet.[5]

Meanwhile, a young child who is expected to read before he is ready to do so easily is put in a stressful situation. He or she may not be able to succeed no matter how hard the child tries. Early failure brings disappointment, discouragement, and damage to a young child's self-esteem.

No Play for Elementary Children

A typical nine-year-old elementary school student may have to work to find time to play. When school is over at 2:30 or 3:30 P.M., other activities such as band, soccer, and science club are just getting started. Somewhere in the day there has to be time for homework. If that same child has to help get dinner ready or be responsible for a younger sibling before Mom or Dad gets home, there is even less time or energy for playing or being creative.

Traditional playtimes during school are also being squeezed out. Recess has been eliminated at many elementary schools in recent years as a waste of valuable instructional time. Child development specialists have known for some time, however, that young children need to get up from their desks occasionally and be physically active. They concentrate better after such a break. With that in mind, some teachers have organized recess.

In one school in our district, kindergarten recess is devoted to structured physical fitness exercises instead of unstructured play.

Television watching has also helped squeeze out play. Before the days of television sets in every home, children had to pass the time doing what for them came naturally—playing together. Now they can pass the time passively watching television. Lost is the physical and emotional stimulation, the opportunity for creativity, that play offers.

It is not that children do not want to play anymore, but that everything and everyone seems to be conspiring against it. Parents know what it takes to get ahead in the world today. It takes a competitive edge, a head start, using every minute, every opportunity.

If you enjoy a good baseball game, one of your most frustrating experiences is watching children try to organize and play baseball spontaneously. Choosing sides seems to take forever and then the rules must be agreed upon. Even then those rules may be peculiar to those children and that one game (if you hit it past the oak tree, you're out!). Often the game will be interrupted for long stretches while each side argues over the application of those rules.

Part of our frustration as adults watching the game would be that the games are so unorganized and they do not follow the rules. Today more and more child's play, which often does appear unorganized and operates by its own rules (the children's rules), is being taken over by adults. The result is that many children's play activities have become highly competitive and success oriented. Little Leagues provide organized, competitive sports for eight and nine year olds. Summer camps offer highly structured, specialized skills training in basketball, soccer, computers, and languages.

Children play because it is fun. It is fun to play with other children. As they play, they learn to get along with those children, also. This kind of play is pleasant and beneficial. Much of the competitive, "winning is the only thing" play that children engage in today is more accurately understood as stressful adult behavior.

It is exactly at this time in life that elementary children need from adults the time and the opportunity "to play their own games, make up their own rules and abide by their own timetables."[6] Without that time and opportunity, valuable social learning and emotional growth are lost.

Play for its own sake does not seem to "fit" anymore. Like recess, it is frivolous, a waste of time. But time is exactly what it takes for a child to discover who he or she is, to develop his or her talents and personality. It takes time to develop that "rich inner life" from which creativity springs. Without time to play, daydream, and reflect on life, a person's inner life remains void, filled by turning on the television for a quick fix of entertainment when bored.[7]

At least one perceptive observer understands how television works against the development of creativity and an inner life in a young child. Rita Kramer characterizes extreme television viewing as a "totally destructive activity for children." This is not necessarily because of the content viewed, but because of the nature of television watching itself. Television watching, she says, "works against every important need of the young child; to be interacting with members of his family, learning about them and himself, to practice skills not only relating to people but in the creative use of his own body and his own imagination; to learn to organize and express his own ideas verbally, . . .to create his own fantasies in order to work out solutions to his problems."[8]

Children do need to play for play's sake, it seems. According to child psychologist David Elkind, pleasurable play provides for children, as well as for adults, an important "stress valve," a way of reducing the normal (and not so normal) stresses on a child.[9]

When adults are deprived of adequate stress relief through lack of leisure time and recreation, the results are all too common: ulcers and stomach disorders, alcohol and chemical abuse, depression, and even suicide. How do children react to stress?

"Drug Users Started at 12, Survey Shows," "Under 15 Suicide

Rate Up Sharply." Those newspaper reports tell the story.[10] Children have come under increasing stress, and have begun to react to it similarly to adults. As children take on adult stresses and adult reactions to stress, they lose more of the special innocence of childhood.

The Dubious Value of a Head Start

The evening news regularly brings us reports of the latest super baby. He is a boy of eighteen months who can pronounce 300 Latin words and count to 100. She is a girl of two and a half years who has a vocabulary of 3000 words and can spell every one of them. Their parents are proud; other parents are envious.

Every parent wants to feel that he or she has done a good job of parenting. Their child's early academic achievement is one clear way to measure that success and to feel as though they have given their child a "head start" on success in this highly competitive society. Whether that is true or not, however, is not at all clear.

Anyone who has ever taught a six-year-old child to memorize a Bible verse knows it can be done. A young child can learn to repeat accurately such a great truth as "For the wages of sin is death, but the gift of God is eternal life in Christ Jesus our Lord."[11] But if you ask that same six-year-old child what "wages," "sin," "death," and "eternal life" mean in the context of that verse, you may find that they "learned" the verse, but have not begun to "understand" it.

This is rote learning only. Preschoolers *can* learn to spell multisyllable words or count into the thousands; just because a two and a half year old can count to ten is no guarantee he or she understands the relationship between the numbers one and ten. Words can be repeated without any understanding of their meaning. Trained parrots do it every day.

The sad part seems to be that, for all the effort expended, much of this early learning is of little lasting value.[12] Much, if not most, of any advantage gained is lost by second or third grade.[13] Any head start quickly evaporates. Meanwhile much time and effort has been spent, much pressure put on the child, and much constructive playtime lost when "the probability is high that (he) will learn it all later anyway, more easily and with understanding."[14]

Children are under growing pressure to achieve and succeed early in life. In that sense childhood is becoming much more like adulthood. The irony is that this pressure on children to achieve may well be self-defeating, working against them developing into happy, well-adjusted, and productive members of society.

A study of children who had been in preschool between 1967 and 1970 raises serious questions about the value of highly structured, academically oriented preschool programs. Some of the children whose school careers were studied through age fifteen had been through highly structured, teacher-directed preschool programs that stressed academic skills development. Other students had been through preschool programs that encouraged more free play and activities matching the students' interests.

The researchers found that the children attending the highly structured, academically oriented preschools committed twice as many crimes by the age of fifteen and participated less often in extracurricular activities. Students in the programs that took a more relaxed, low-pressure, play-oriented approach committed fewer crimes and used drugs less often than the other group.[15]

This study supports teachers' perceptions that the vital social and emotional development of preschool, kindergarten, and elementary children is suffering under the pressure for academic achievement.[16] It raises serious questions about the long-term impact on both children and society in general.

Let's say it again: Pressure on young children to succeed academically beyond what comes readily and easily to them is likely to be both self-defeating and harmful to children. A child who senses that his or her worth lies primarily in the ability to succeed has a fragile self-image indeed. He or she is in danger of losing exactly what is most crucial to childhood.

> Emotional development is the base for future cognitive success. If a child develops a good sense of himself and his competence in all areas, he will be ready to acquire cognitive competence later on. . . . An emotionally fulfilled child will also have enough self image to care about others and be ready to give to others as well as to acquire for himself. Our society may need a serious re-evaluation—are we raising children to be highly individualistic, intellectually driven and self motivated?—to the exclusion of caring about others around them. Do we want to create cognitive monsters?[17]

Children need time and permission from adults to learn to relate to others as well as to read, to be in touch with their feelings as well as to count, to learn to care about others, and to give as well as receive from them, just as much as they need to learn to write. These things touch the very life of faith. Are they not ultimately more important than a high I.Q.?

Children are rapidly losing the gift of a playful, unpressured childhood where they can learn how to live. Instead the adult goal of success (pursued in competition with others) has come to dominate childhood also.[18]

What *is* a successful child? Is it a child who graduates first in every class and shows promise of being able to help the American economy beat back competition from the Japanese (all the while suffering through addiction to alcohol and three failed marriages)? What are the criteria for judging a successful childhood?

Dolores Curran, a family specialist, asked the question, "What is a successful child?" to a broad selection of parents. They gave her two types of responses. One group of parents believed a successful child is one who achieves much as a child and becomes a successful adult. The bottom line was success.

There was another response given, however. The second group valued their children as children. They put qualities such as self-esteem, carefreeness, and the ability to get along with others ahead of achievements.[19] Their children are more fortunate than most today. They will be encouraged to play, to dream, to develop an inner life, and to be children for as long as they need to be in order to grow up.

Carrying Adult-Sized Burdens

A nineteenth-century French toy manufacturer engraved his understanding of childhood innocence on the toys he made. His description of childhood sounds uncomfortably naive and unrealistic today:

> This is the age of innocence, to which we must all return in order to enjoy the happiness to come which is our hope on earth: the age when one can forgive anything, the age when hatred is unknown, when nothing can cause distress, the golden age of human life, the age which defies Hell, the age when life is easy and death holds no terrors, the age to which the heavens are open. Let tender and gentle respect be shown to these young plants of the church. Heaven is full of anger for whosoever scandalizes them.[20]

This talk of a "golden age" to be preserved at the risk of heaven's anger is a bit romantic, perhaps, yet it captures well the view of childhood innocence that held sway in American culture through much of the first half of this century. This age of innocence "when life is easy and death holds no terrors" was maintained by adults who, it was clear to any young child, held the secrets that allowed adults to control the world in such a way that "nothing could cause distress." And these adults could, on the whole, be trusted to do so.

Surely the world must look different to a child of the present. Today there is much distress caused to children who must bear burdens that are often more appropriate to adolescents and adults: sexuality, separation and loss, and adult responsibilities. A child raised in the 1950s might have faced *some* of these same stresses (though less routinely and with the likelihood of facing only one during his childhood), but not many or all of them as is often the case today.

It has always been a sad fact that divorces happen and parents die. Sons and daughters have had to leave school early to help with the family business. But in the face of these problems, they had an additional asset: They believed that the world they were soon to enter was basically a good and hopeful place controlled by benevolent and trustworthy adult authority figures. Children of the past could maintain this innocent, naive trust in the world of adults well into later elementary or early adolescent years because adults felt it appropriate and even necessary to protect children from premature exposure to many of the foibles, frustrations, and problems of adult life.

At the present time, however, this is no longer true. Today all adult propensities, passions, and perversions, all dilemmas and difficulties are revealed to the younger child. Indeed it is probably true that, as a result, today's child is the "victim of overwhelming stress."[21] Much of the blame for this situation goes to television.

Early in 1987 the evening news in Pittsburgh and Philadelphia played a shocking and grisly film. A state official convicted of taking a kickback was shown putting a loaded gun into his mouth and pulling the trigger as the cameras rolled. The film played during the dinner hour while many families watched.

Each evening the television news brings to the eyes and ears of children of all ages fresh reminders that life can be short and brutal. Children die of starvation and AIDS. Rape, child abuse, and multiple acts of violence are reported in graphic detail. Governmental leaders are accused of all sorts of ineptitude and dishonesty.

Later the news is followed by the evening sitcoms and soaps. They reveal to all viewers, regardless of age, the mysteries and pain of adult passion, conflict, and violence. The combined impact on a child of a couple of hours of watching the evening news and the nightly soaps is that ". . . every variety of adult sexuality, every permutation and combination of human brutality and violence, every aspect of sickness and disease and suffering, every frightening possibility of natural and man-made disaster" that could possibly undermine childhood innocence is revealed to all the six-, seven-, and eight-year-old children watching and all in living color![22]

Television exacts a significant price from a young child's developing moral sensitivities. Harvard professor and child specialist Robert Coles feels that young children of even five or six years have keen moral sensitivities and can notice hypocrisy and moral inconsistencies in the adult world.

On the widely debated topic of the effect of television and violence on children, Coles feels that the real impact is made by the direction in which television pushes a child's moral thinking. The effect of television is not to encourage children to examine issues reflectively and to develop moral sensitivities, but rather to push their thinking toward the same violence, meanness, and exploitation which they see on television.[23]

Television's impact on younger children is heightened by the fact that the material it presents is immediately available to them and to anyone of any age. A young child does not need to be able to read to gain access to the material on television. He or she merely sits and watches, thereby being exposed to many experiences previously considered the province of adults.

Most commercial television programming (with the notable and dubious exception of Saturday morning) is prepared with adult viewers in mind. Advertisers want to capture the urban, middle-class audience ranging in age from eighteen to forty-nine years old. This is the group with the disposable income advertisers want to attract. Hence, programs are produced by adults for adults and feature adult violence and sexual situations.

The so-called family hour, from eight to nine in the evening, has not been very successful in providing more family-oriented entertainment. Filling that hour are usually "crime and punishment" series, featuring stories revolving around acts of violence, or sitcoms that often deal with the love lives of adults. Even if this hour were rigidly programmed with more appropriate material for children, the impact would be slight. Many upper elementary age children simply do not go to bed at nine o'clock any more, and certainly not on weekends!

Television has given young children access to the world of adult experiences that was never before so fully available to them. Preserving a child's innocent ignorance of adult problems and passions has never been easy, but in the past parents were convinced it was necessary and that it was their duty to their children to preserve this innocence as best they could.

The past two decades seem to show a dramatic shift away from protecting childhood innocence and toward allowing or even promoting the exposure of children to the burdens of adulthood. Some of this may simply be a recognition of the dominance of television in our culture. Some may result from the belief that in a complex, rapidly changing world full of dangers for children and adolescents, the more a child learns at a younger age, the better prepared for life he or she will be.[24]

Certainly the exposure of preadolescent children to the adult world makes children *appear* more grown up and sophisticated earlier in life. But this pressure to grow up faster and be prepared for life inevitably exacts a price from a child's spirit. Though they are pushed and invited by society to take on adult perspectives and thus to grow up more quickly, the effect may be the opposite. Unlike their predecessors who could not wait to grow up, young children today may be in no hurry at all, perhaps may even be afraid of becoming adults. They have to wonder what kind of world they are being pushed to enter.

As one observer put it, "This is the real loss of innocence; losing the implicit belief that the world is a good and stable place in which to live."[25] If adults cannot be trusted to control their impulses to violence, passion, and aggression, a child can quickly lose that implicit optimism and faith in the goodness of the world that so characterizes childhood innocence.

There is a brief but wonderful time for parents in the life of every young child when the child really believes that parents (and other adults too) know everything and are always right. This is a fantasy, to be sure, and one that children discard all too quickly! But it is a useful fantasy and not just for harried parents.

As that fantasy is maintained through the early elementary years, a young child is given the emotional security he or she needs to develop a sense of trust in the basic goodness and trustworthiness of adult authority figures. The child can then develop a sense of trust in the adult world and a sense of optimism about his or her future life as an adult.

Further, child development specialists agree that children have a real need to see adults clearly in control of their lives and impulses. They need to see adult authority figures, such as parents and Sunday school teachers, who have a clear concept of right and wrong. As the child sees adults who are important to him or her controlling their own behavior on the basis of clear moral values, he or she is able to model after them in developing his or her own values and self-discipline.[26] Thus the child is able to make moral choices and act in a disciplined way.

A child born in 1980 has surely cast aside that useful fantasy by now. Television has shown time and again that adults cannot control themselves. Subtle but clear messages from all around tell the child that right and wrong are not always clear, if they exist at all. Under these circumstances it becomes difficult for an elementary child to acquire two of the most important aspects of a productive adult (and Christian) life: self-discipline and a clear set of moral values.

Playing at Being Grown Up

One of the Saturday afternoon television shows in our area is called "Puttin' on the Kids" (an unintended pun, I'm sure). This show features children as young as six or seven and rarely older than twelve, lip-synching the words of and dancing to their favorite pop songs. The children are judged and awarded prizes on how well they imitate their favorite rock stars dancing, gesturing, and expressing their feelings about the words of the song. Most of the songs, of course, deal with boy-girl relationships.

These kids really are being "put on." They are being encouraged to leave childhood behind, grow up quickly, and imitate a level of emotional and physical maturity well beyond their years. They may, in fact, look and act like young adults, but emotionally they remain children.

As Neil Postman demonstrates so clearly in his book *The Disappearance of Childhood*, television is the main influence in mixing and confusing the worlds of adults and children.[27] But there are other influences as well.

At least through the sixteenth century, children were dressed like adults of their social class.[28] Then, as a lengthened period of childhood evolved, children were differentiated from adults by their own special clothing. Young boys wore knickers; trousers were for men. Little girls had distinctive dresses and hairstyles of their own.

By the mid-1960s, however, distinctive clothing as a marker of childhood was beginning to change. Jeans and sneakers, once exclusively the clothing of children, began to be worn widely by adults. Preadolescent girls, spurred on by television ads during the Saturday morning cartoons, began to clamor to wear makeup previously reserved for women.

Not surprisingly, once young children are allowed and encouraged to dress like adults, they will be encouraged to act like adults. Perhaps the air of sophistication an eleven or twelve year old can acquire from watching the prime-time soaps and the evening news makes it easier for adults to believe that these children are more grown up than their age (at least in knowledge, if not also in understanding and judgment).

A church near our home sponsors a monthly dance to which eleven and twelve year olds are invited. Such activities are common in churches and schools today. Only a generation ago children of their age would not be interested (or encouraged to be interested) in boy-girl relationships. They would be expected to be off playing somewhere (in single-sex groups)!

As play disappears today, children are often encouraged to engage in activities once considered more appropriate for adolescents and adults. The results are not surprising. Early boy-girl interaction encourages early dating, and early dating leads to early sex.

A recent study found that 91 percent of girls who began dating at age twelve had intercourse before graduation from high school. Of those who began at age sixteen, only 20 percent had sex before they graduated.[29] When encouraged to begin to act like grown-ups at an early age, children do just that!

Inevitably, children pay a price for the loss of their innocence as they are pushed prematurely out of childhood. David Elkind observes that "hurrying" young children into adult life, however well intentioned, can produce many fears, angers, and anxieties. Children are forced to confront the issues and problems of adulthood before they have finished being children. They are robbed of the time and energy that they can devote to self-discovery and to constructing a set of values that give meaning to their lives, both as children and later as adults.[30]

Growth into personhood in our complex, complicated society takes time. It takes time for children to finish the major tasks of childhood—understanding their world and learning how to live successfully in it. It takes perhaps even more time, not less, than in previous generations.

If the relatively long period of growth and development that childhood affords is too severely shortened, these tasks must be left unfinished. Pushing children prematurely into adolescence and adulthood robs them of the time they need to build a healthy sense of their own competence, self-esteem, and trust in the world they live in. These qualities are the building blocks of lifelong emotional and spiritual health.[31]

"The child is father to the man," poet William Wordsworth said. He is also father to the parent. The child who grows up deprived of self-esteem and a sense of competence finds it difficult to care for others, even his or her own children. The child's own spirit is shrunken, and he or she finds it hard as a parent, to nourish the spirit of his or her own children.

Preparation for parenthood begins with feeling loved, feeling a sense of adequacy, as a child. Children who are allowed time to develop these feelings rarely need to satisfy their own needs by pressuring their children to achieve. They rarely become abusive parents. Rather, from the deep well of their own spirits, they pass on gifts of unconditional love, a sense of trust and caring for others that is the foundation of emotional and spiritual wholeness.

These "successful parents" build into their children the basis for true success in all areas of life. The gift of a sense of worth and competence means freedom to live guided by "whatever is true, whatever is noble, whatever is right, whatever is pure, whatever is lovely,"[32] not by what people will think. The child is given the freedom to live without suspicion of authority, whether religious or governmental, and the freedom to care about the welfare of others. Children who enter adulthood with these gifts offer much to the society in which they live and to the faith to which they give their allegiance.

Guiding the Boat Themselves

If Thomas Cole were painting today, he would have to depict childhood differently. Many children today are no longer granted that relaxed, playful voyage of innocence through childhood, guided and sheltered by adults. Rather by the mid-elementary years, they are asked to begin to guide the boat; they are expected to grow up quickly, cast off their innocence, and take up many of the burdens of adult life.

As great as the impact of all this surely is on the emotional and psychological growth of children, the moral and spiritual impact is even greater. The Christian faith is a realistic faith that recognizes the reality of sin, evil, and suffering as a fact of life for all people. But it is also a faith of hope: the sure hope of the final triumph over sin and suffering won by Jesus Christ. It is an optimistic faith. This optimism is born of faith in the promise that all things "work together for good to those who love God."[33]

In previous generations children grew up with a certain naive hopefulness about life, an "I can't wait to grow up" optimism. As they matured, their naiveté became realism. But although the innocent hopefulness that infused their spirit may have been tempered over time, its essence remained with them as they grew. That hopefulness provided an element congenial to the growth of Christian faith.

Children who have had the gift of growing up in a family and a society where adults saw to it that all, or at least most, things *did* work together for good have little trouble believing that biblical promise. Intuitively, it makes sense. But the loss of childhood innocence undermines this optimism about the future and makes it much more difficult for children today to embrace this hopeful, optimistic faith.

Marie Winn correctly points out the connection between the decline in respect for adult authority and the diminished respect for the authority of religion. Children form their attitudes toward the authority of a God they cannot see from interactions with adults they can see. If parents, teachers, and government leaders are not trustworthy, not "in control," not morally consistent, and not available when needed, a child's understanding of God's trustworthiness, His ability to care for the child, and His benevolent authority will all be severely warped.

If you cannot trust God, whom can you trust? At some point in every Christian's life, there are no answers. One must exercise trust in the authority of God; one must walk by faith. The loss of innocent childhood trust in adult authority makes the mature development of this trust in God's authority much more difficult.[34]

The loss of childhood innocence and the ability to trust and depend on adults strikes at the heart of the child's spirit. Jesus commended that trusting, dependent spirit to adults as a model of faith: "Except you repent and *become as little children*, you cannot see the Kingdom of Heaven." As childhood innocence is lost, adults lose this living, breathing model of what their own innocent, trusting faith is to be like.

The loss of childhood innocence has crushed the spirits of many young children today. Having eaten of the fruit of the tree of the knowledge of adulthood, they have been expelled from the garden of childhood and sent out alone into the frightening world of adults.[35] There, worried and vulnerable, these children have heard confusing yet enticing whispers of the oldest and most mysterious of adult secrets, the secret of sex. For them, innocence is lost and childhood is over.

THREE:

The Loss
of Sexual Secrecy

In 1983 pop star Linda Ronstadt began recording love songs
from the 1920s, 1930s, and 1940s. Most were wistful ballads
of hope for romance or of despair at its loss. To listeners
accustomed to the pop songs of the 1980s, these must have
sounded almost childlike in their treatment of love and romance.

What is missing from most of these ballads is hardly a hint of
adult sexuality. Oblique, indirect public references to sex were
acceptable during that period, but nothing more. Sex was a
private matter, a dark (or at least gray) secret not appropriate for
public discussion and certainly not to be discussed within earshot
of children.

By 1970, however, pop music was becoming much more open
in discussing adult sexual impulses. Popular songs with sexually
explicit lyrics became standard fare on pop radio stations and the
trend has continued to the present. What would have never
entered the mind of a ten-year-old child in the 1950s can hardly
be hidden in the 1980s.

Sex had been, at least for the past 150 years, one of the most
closely guarded of adult secrets. The modern view of childhood
has been defined, at least partially, by an understanding of the
value of protecting children from the knowledge of adult
sexuality.[1] When children were present, sex was a dirty little
secret to be kept just that, a secret.

Indeed, this conspiracy of silence has been said to be a basic
civilizing feature of our culture. Sexual impulses must be

channeled and controlled if society is to survive. One means of control is to "privatize" the sexual impulse (and its expression). A direct effect of this privatization has been to keep sexual knowledge secret and away from children.[2] Today, however, the secret is out. The message is publicly displayed to people of all ages on television talk shows and sitcoms, on billboards and popular magazines, and on the radio.

Surgeon General C. Everett Koop has recommended that children in third grade (as young as seven years old) receive graphic sex education instruction in hopes of slowing the spread of AIDS.[3] Many children will find that information frightening, confusing, and overwhelming, to say the least.

Postponing the time when children encounter the knowledge of adult sexuality helps prolong childhood. They do not worry about the risks of homosexual relations. They can just be children. A price must be paid when a young child confronts adult sex and has to wrestle with the challenges it presents. When this happens, as Anna Freud said, a child's self-confidence can easily be shattered and normal emotional and psychological growth arrested.[4]

It is not surprising, for instance, that marriages between adolescents are susceptible to an even higher divorce rate than marriages in general. When they are forced to put childhood behind them prematurely, they must leave undone much of the "business" of childhood. They do not have the time for their moral and emotional development to catch up with their physical and cognitive development. They enter marriage and family relationships emotionally and spiritually underdeveloped.

If they have been victims of the flood of pornography and child sexual abuse washing over the country, their own attitudes and values toward sex and marriage will be severely warped. Often their adolescence and adulthood will be spent painfully and needlessly relearning the lessons of prior generations. They will be doomed to wander through the wilderness of casual sex, never to reach the promised land of committed love and emotional as well as physical intimacy.

It is no longer widely accepted that early exposure to adult sexual impulses and activities is harmful or even inappropriate for young children. One observer has defined children as a group of people who do not know certain things that adults know, especially concerning sex.[5] At least it used to be that way. Every parent knows all too well that "little pitchers have big ears." Children can and do often hear more than their parents wish! But the growth of literacy in the latter nineteenth and early twentieth century meant that sexual knowledge could not be kept from children just by being put in books.[6]

In the 1950s and 1960s, a high school library commonly had a "restricted section" of books behind the librarian's desk or in a special room. Books kept there could be checked out only by seniors and sometimes only with parental permission. Public librarians saw to it that sexually explicit classics such as Chaucer's *Canterbury Tales* or D.H. Lawrence's *Lady Chatterley's Lover* were carefully guarded from the gaze of young children. All were restricted for the same reason, the use of sexually crude language and explicit sexuality. These were deemed inappropriate for children and young adolescents.

Adults already knew the information contained in those "adult" books. But children weren't considered sufficiently self-disciplined or emotionally mature enough to deal with full exposure to adult sexuality. So children and adolescents were kept in the dark as much as possible (and restrained from sexual activity by social expectations and values) until they were judged ready to be initiated gradually into the mysteries of sex and the moral values that insured its greatest enjoyment.

Those of us who grew up in the 1950s and 1960s knew well that some of our high school classmates were telling the truth when they bragged about "scoring" in the car at the drive-in. But we also knew they were a distinct minority. Our admiration for their entry into this forbidden territory was tempered by disgust at their breaking the rule: no sex before marriage.

By the 1980s, this situation had changed radically. Teens have always been sexually active, but usually in smaller numbers.

Today the United States has the highest teen pregnancy rate of any industrialized nation. Teens date earlier, have sex earlier, get pregnant earlier, and get married earlier. Consequently, they get divorced earlier, as the statistics on teen marriages show.

"A little knowledge is a dangerous thing" one of my high school teachers always said, especially in the hands of the young. Often, she insisted we knew just enough about something to misuse it (be dangerous), but not enough to treat it properly. This is the situation facing many children and adolescents today. To Americans, knowledge has one overriding purpose: to be acted upon. Armed with sexual knowledge, children and adolescents today are acting accordingly.

The Beginning of the End

"No more between the lines. Tonight's between the sheets." That was the caption on a large advertisement in a national daily newspaper for a long-awaited episode of the popular evening television series *Moonlighting*. David and Maddie were finally going to go to bed together "after 2½ years of foreplay," as one reviewer described it.

That show aired at 9:00 P.M. in the East but earlier in the Midwest, and could be seen by young children and adolescents. Many preadolescent children routinely stay up later than 9:00 P.M. on school nights. Beginning in the 1950s with its gradual entry into nearly every home, television has become the primary source of exposure of children to adult sexual secrets. What once could be kept secret in adult books is now openly displayed on the family TV screen.

In the earliest days of television, producers were forbidden by network policy from acknowledging adult sexuality. Television could not show couples in bed together, even if fully clothed in pajamas and sitting up reading! Lucille Ball (Lucy) could not even mention the word *pregnant* in her popular series, "I Love Lucy." These network policies reflected a larger social consensus, still alive in the 1950s, that sex was both a private (not for public discussion) and an adult matter (not for discussion in the presence of children).

Since the 1960s, television's impact has converged with and influenced the growth of the sexual revolution and the accompanying decline of sex as an adult-only topic. The omnipresence of television has made it virtually impossible to keep sexual secrets from preadolescent children today.

The greater openness about sexual matters that began in the 1960s and carried on through the 1970s continued to lead to the breaking of new ground on television in the 1980s. Such widely seen early evening shows as "Facts of Life" and "Diff'rent Strokes" attempted to be family comedies featuring children and adolescents at the center of the story lines.

These and similar shows, however, often discussed ongoing affairs by parents and other adult characters. They even featured plots based on the parents' premarital sexual experiences. Furthermore, afternoon soap operas and talk shows, the evening news, and prime time specials all discuss homosexuality, rape, incest, and child abuse. The afternoon soaps are notoriously steamy in plot and action, showing "constant and irresponsible sexual behavior: no waiting, very few morals."[7] From a news standpoint, the sexual habits and preferences of public figures are fair game for discussion on the public airwaves.

Watching television only during the so-called family hour (8:00 to 9:00 P.M. EST) is no guarantee that a child will avoid the on-air depiction and discussion of adult sexuality. An episode of "My Sister Sam," a CBS sitcom aired during the family hour, contained a discussion between Sam and her younger sister Patti in which Sam revealed that she was embarrassed to have sex with her boyfriend (from out of town) while Patti slept in the next room. She solved her problem, she explained to Patti, by sleeping with her boyfriend in a local hotel.

Another popular CBS sitcom, "Kate and Allie," once featured a conversation where Allie's daughter, Jenny, had been caught on the way to bed with her boyfriend. Allie's concern, it turned out, focused on Jenny's awareness and use of contraceptives (not the advisability of the relationship itself!)[8] The list could go on, of course. The ABC sitcom "Who's the Boss?" starring Tony Danza regularly featured sexual innuendoes and jokes.

It is true that some, but by no means the majority, of the most offensive television programs such as risqué talk and variety shows are shown late at night (or at least after 10:00 P.M.). However, statistics indicate that on any given night about 3 million children between the ages of two and eleven years are watching television between 11:00 to 11:30 P.M. The figure is still at 2 million between 12:30 and 1:00 A.M.! Even between 1:00 and 1:30 A.M. there are nearly three-quarters of a million children watching television![9] The 8:00 to 9:00 P.M. family hour does not offer them a lot of protection, does it?

Keeping sexual information from children allows them to finish the business of growing up emotionally and physically without the added burden of confronting this adult challenge. It also allows adults to introduce children to sexual matters in a controlled manner, in the context of growing bodies, growing emotions, and growing moral sensitivities.

Even if, as critics allege, the sex education offered by parents was haphazard at best, it tended to come when needed (and not much earlier). Also, children had the benefit of a larger moral consensus in a society that, by and large, provided clear guidelines for sexual expression. Today children are caught in a double bind: They know more earlier in life when they are less equipped emotionally to manage their sexuality, and the moral guidelines they so desperately need are largely lacking!

Even more harmful than this early exposure to sex is the context within which these secrets are revealed. Rarely, if ever, is sex portrayed in the context of a long-term, fulfilling marriage relationship. Rather, children are more likely to see adult sex portrayed as uncontrollable lust and passion that is normally satisfied whenever and with whomever possible.

Actors and television executives alike find the content of their shows fully justified. A CBS vice-president for programming was quoted as saying "It's not a 'Green Acres' world anymore. There has simply been a loss of innocence in society across the board and television reflects this."[10] Indeed, the networks broadcast only what they are reasonably certain is acceptable to most Americans (witness the heated debate over television advertising of condoms).

One early evening sitcom star defended her sexual, innuendo-filled show by saying "It's a mistake to think young people don't know anything about sex or sexual innuendo." Her niece, nephews, and the young people she works with say and know things "that make (her) hair stand on end." Most script-writers, actors, and television executives would probably agree with her enthusiastically.

We would be foolish, she insisted, to think that adolescents (and even children) don't know about sex and don't enjoy a little teasing and joking about it.[11] Perhaps we *are* foolish. But such a situation can hardly be applauded. Sex is now an open secret and, having lost its shroud of secrecy, it has also lost much of the awe and dignity due it as a great and powerful gift of the Creator to His creation. As a result, children will inherit a cheapened, tawdry, and devalued gift.

If Phillippe Aries, a French historian of family life and childhood, were writing about contemporary America, surely he would be shocked. What he called that "strictest and most respected" law of contemporary morality that required adults of previous generations to avoid any sexual references, especially humorous ones, in the presence of children, is now better characterized as "loosest and largely neglected."[12]

Television is not the sole culprit. It would be quite possible to do as extensive (and depressing) an examination of movies available to young children today. In the 1950s almost any American film was suitable for viewing by children. The motion picture producer lived by codes that did not permit nudity, rape, explicit sex, or excessive violence to be portrayed on screen. As Marie Winn observes, adults knew well what movies could *not* show and acted in ways movies could *not* portray. For the sake of their children's innocence, however, they accepted a sexual blackout imposed on movies. Sexual secrets were largely kept secret. Today, however, movies have also let the secret out. As a result, children now know what once they could only suspect. [13]

Adolescent "sexploitation" movies are common in a film studio's repertoire today. Movies routinely feature crude sexual humor, teenage boys squinting through peepholes into girls' locker rooms and showers, and frequent attempts by adolescent couples to "make it" on camera.

The fact that these films are usually rated PG (Parental Guidance Suggested) or PG-13 (Some Material May Not Be Suitable for Children Under 13) is of little consolation. Children of any age who can pay the price of admission have open access to these films and to the frivolous, exploitative, immature, and harmful attitudes and values about sexual relationships that they convey.

The Sexual Child

A famous maker of jeans recently produced a television commercial depicting elementary age children posing and acting in sexually provocative ways. The commercial attracted some attention (the company's aim, no doubt), but the fact that it was shown at all, points to another startling consequence of the loss of sexual secrecy: the emergence of the sexual child.

Children have more sexual knowledge at a younger age than in the previous two centuries. As a result, even preadolescent children today can appear sexually sophisticated, both in the language they use and the topics they discuss. Since for most adults sexual knowledge is gained to be acted on, many adults assume a sexually knowledgeable child is probably a sexually active child.

If this great openness about sexual matters can be called the sexual revolution, then a second, even more tragic, sexual revolution is now in progress. Its central characteristic is this radical shift in adult attitudes toward childhood sexuality, a shift away from seeing children as sexually innocent and toward portraying them as acceptable objects of adult sexual desire.

A generation ago children were assumed to be largely innocent of the knowledge of adult sexuality until puberty forced the issue. But as children have changed, adult attitudes toward children and their sexuality have also changed. Today early adolescent children, and sometimes even preadolescents, are expected to be sexual in ways previously thought impossible or inappropriate. Consequently, they have become sex objects themselves.

The media have both fostered and exploited this dangerous change in attitudes toward children. One particularly shocking magazine ad for men's clothing featured a casually well-dressed young man, probably in his mid-twenties. A naked young girl, who appeared to be about ten, was standing behind him. What was the message of that ad? Do well-dressed young men desire ten-year-old girls? Or do ten-year-old girls desire well-dressed twenty-five-year-old men?

Actress Brooke Shields has been a central character in the media exploitation of child sexuality. She was photographed in the nude at ten years of age. Later, the photos were sold for a significant sum and published. A generation ago the public distribution of those photos would have been judged highly inappropriate, at the least.

This new social attitude toward the sexual nature of children has helped to weaken those good and necessary social restraints on adult-child sexual interaction. The result has been a tragedy for children in two particularly disturbing areas: sexual abuse of children and the flourishing of child pornography.

As many as 40 million men and women today have been victims of sexual abuse (ranging from fondling to intercourse) as children. Most abuse occurs between the ages of nine and twelve years old when the psychological effects of the "shattered innocence" of the child are the greatest.[14]

It may be too strong to say that the current image of sexual children has significantly increased child sexual abuse. Nonetheless, as long as children are portrayed in both visual and print media as sexually aware and provocative, that is, as long as they are commercially sexually exploited, sexual abuse of children is likely to increase.

Commercial, sexual exploitation of children, especially girls, reflects and encourages further abuse and exploitation by bringing "out of the closet" and helping to legitimize one of the darkest and dirtiest of adult sexual secrets: that men find young girls sexually stimulating. A generation ago when Vladimir Nabokov wrote about twelve-year-old Lolita sleeping with Humbert Humbert, the public reaction was disgust and revulsion. One must wonder if such a novel would draw much attention if published today.

One of the functions of sexual secrecy has always been preservation of the sexual relationship itself. Keeping sexual activity private grew out of a recognition that it was essentially an act nourished and best effectuated within a context of intimacy and privacy. Public display and discussion of sex alters the character of sex in a detrimental way. That which the Creator intended to be special and intimate becomes cheapened and common.

The loss of secrecy and thus of sexual privacy also has consequences for marriage. The sense of the sacred is lost. The awesome, almost sacramental character of the "one flesh" act of marriage is cheapened when it becomes a topic of everyday discussion and depiction. That relationship that the Creator intended to reflect Christ's relationship to His church has been cheapened and trivialized.[15]

Secrecy helps regulate sexual behavior. Before the sexual revolution, homosexual behavior was neither widely accepted nor discussed openly. Premarital and extramarital sex were treated similarly. Once they became common topics of public discussion, they became less secret, less shameful, and more legitimate.

In the past this combination of shame and secrecy has played a powerful restraining function on adult sexual activities, especially those involving children. The loss of secrecy and the subsequent change in the attitudes of adults toward children pose some real dangers.

As the second sexual revolution progresses and adults accept the idea of the sexual child, we can expect to see a gradual regression to the situation children faced in the Middle Ages. Contemporary accounts of social life in the sixteenth century indicate that intimate physical contact and fondling of children's genitals (especially of boys) were common and entirely permissible.[16] Today's widespread abuse against young girls parallels sixteenth-century practices.

The second sexual revolution has led to a serious loosening of many of the traditional restraints on adult sexual activity involving children. Nowhere is this more tragically evident than in the flourishing child pornography industry.

Child pornography is a multimillion dollar illegal industry trading on the sexual exploitation of children. It is a logical, if horrible, extension of the social attitude now permitting the sexual exploitation of children in the visual and print media. The "Final Report of the Attorney General's Commission on Pornography," issued in 1986, condemns child pornography not simply because it is pornography but because it represents a particularly harmful form of sexual exploitation and sexual abuse of young children and adolescents.

The bulk of child pornography consists of pictures of actual children, often preschool or early elementary age, photographed while engaged in some sexual activity with an adult or another child. These pictures are sold to magazines that are published abroad. The Attorney General's report points out, however, that the majority of their readers and contributors are Americans.

Child pornography is not just a harmless or distasteful fascination, as some have suggested. There is significant evidence, the report states, that photographs of children engaged in sexual activity are used to "soften up" children (by showing them that other children do it) for subsequent molestation.[17]

The shattered innocence of young children caused by this abuse would be serious enough by itself; the psychological havoc wreaked on children by pedophiles is even more terrible. A young child feels worthless, cheap, and guilty after such exploitation. These feelings can last a lifetime, crippling a child's self-esteem and his or her attempts to maintain mature and loving adult relationships.

Child pornography is now generally recognized as repugnant and socially dangerous. The United States Congress outlawed the use of minors (under the age of eighteen) in pornography in the Child Protection Act of 1984. State and local efforts against child pornography are also gaining momentum.

But child pornography is only part of a much larger problem affecting children and adults alike: the toleration of the pornography industry in general. The sexual revolution that fostered the loss of sexual secrecy and accompanied the weakening of the traditional Christian moral context for sex has created conditions in which pornography of any kind can flourish.

As long as there is no public outcry against the pornography industry, government enforcement of antipornography laws will remain minimal and the pornography industry will continue to flourish.

As long as the pornography industry flourishes, pornography will continue to find its way into children's hands and minds, whether through cable television, videos, or "men's magazines" left around the house. "Dial-a-porn" telephone services, which in my city have distributed their advertising leaflets in the streets around elementary schools, will continue to play sexually explicit messages for any child old enough to dial a telephone.

As long as the pornography industry flourishes, children of eleven, twelve, and thirteen, just beginning to discover their emerging sexuality, will also have to deal with violent, harmful, and degrading attitudes toward adult sexuality. They will see the "raw power" of sex without the benefit of the Christian moral context that permits them to see its wonderful beauty.

As long as the pornography industry flourishes, adolescent

attitudes toward women, marriage, and family will continue to be distorted by this material. Children will continue to be abused and exploited, their bodies and spirits bruised and shattered. The consequences for the spiritual and emotional health of an entire generation of children are frightening indeed.

No Reason to Say No

The first sexual revolution produced a public tolerance and even an appetite for open discussion and depiction of sexual matters. The second sexual revolution is producing a dangerous change in adult attitudes toward children that can only lead to growing child sexual abuse and exploitation. It is time for a third sexual revolution.

The third sexual revolution must be led by concerned Christian adults and others who share their values about sex. It must be a revolution fought on behalf of children.

"Human sexuality is a moral issue in every society," says Harvard psychology professor Jerome Kagan. "But while some societies have a consensus on sex, ours doesn't."[18] Therein, as the playwright said, lies the rub.

The sexual revolution of the 1960s was the beginning of the end for the dominant social consensus in America about sex. This consensus, following broad biblical guidelines, upheld the values of sex within marriage (only), marital fidelity and stability, and the "awe-ful" quality of sex. Linked to this appreciation of the special nature of sex was a reticence to discuss or display it publicly. Television and other popular media (with some obvious exceptions) generally conformed to these general guidelines.

The result was a general but clear set of social values and expectations about sex that guided the conduct both of children and adults. These expectations, rooted in the biblical heritage of the country, formed a strong fence around the minefield of adult sexuality that both prohibited children from getting in and prohibited adults from getting sexually involved with children.

This social consensus provided these benefits because it was both widely and generally accepted and because the values and expectations that adults had for their children's sexuality largely matched those they had for their own. Certainly there have always been philanderers and fallen women as they were euphemistically called, but their conduct was generally condemned as wrong.

The erosion of that social consensus has presented many adults with an additional problem: They want to have unrestrained sexual activity for themselves while shielding their children from the current plague of teenage pregnancies and out of wedlock births. They have found that it just won't work.

Since the 1960s the sexual revolution has gradually eroded social restraints on sexual activity. For children, there is no longer strong support for resisting the pressure when everybody's doing it or when someone says "if you love me, you'll do it." For adults, the social sanctions against child sexual exploitation, though still in place (witness strong laws against child pornography), are clearly endangered. Children have lost the invaluable benefits of a strong social consensus built on a biblical understanding of sex as an intimate and private wonder intended for married adults only. That loss robs children of any good reason to say no to sex.

With no reason to abstain from sex, we should not be surprised that many children (yes, children) and teens don't. More than 1 million teenage American girls become pregnant each year, most by teenage boys. Approximately 125,000 of those pregnant girls are younger than fifteen.[19]

Current studies show that by the time they reach twenty, 81 percent of today's unmarried young men and 60 percent of unmarried young women will experience sexual intercourse. More shocking is that half of today's sexually involved young men had their first sexual experiences between the ages of eleven and thirteen.[20] Children, it seems, are caught up in the sexual revolution in more ways than one. They are certainly its saddest casualties.

What About Sex Education?

Advocates of sex education in the public schools quote evidence that sex education courses in junior and senior high school help to lower adolescent sexual activity and pregnancy.[21] Others would establish school-based health clinics in public schools to distribute birth control aids to the students. This way, at least, pregnancies can be reduced.

Is sex education in public schools, perhaps combined with school-based health clinics, the solution? Noted child psychologist Bruno Bettelheim asserts what many parents suspect: Sex education in public schools is itself a factor in the *increase* in teenage sex and pregnancies.[22]

Sex education in the public schools as currently presented is doomed to failure. The assumption underlying most sex education (and the school-based health clinics) is that teenagers cannot be self-disciplined in the area of sex. Their sexual activity is assumed to be inevitable.

Teachers and parents have known for years that children tend to live up (or down) to the expectations held of them. It has been proven in the classroom; now it is being proven in the bedroom. Children do what is expected of them and sex is no exception.

Adults, of course, do not help the situation. The message children get from billboards, television shows, and commercials is clear: If it feels good, do it. Because they are unwilling to model self-discipline and respect for marital sex in their own lives, many adults help transform their expectations of the inevitability of teenage sex into reality.

Some sex education classes are based on a values clarification approach. Thus they boil down to asking the child to decide what he or she thinks is right in this situation. Other courses aim at assisting in the sexual adjustment of sexually active teens or in helping them be more sensitive to their partners' needs while enjoying sex as a normal and natural part of life. These sex education programs must indeed appear to many teens to be condoning, if not advocating, teenage sex.[23]

Sex education in the public schools is doomed to failure because it cannot be "value neutral." Children and adolescents need a clear, consistent message as to their parents' and teachers' expectations for their sexuality. The current controversy over sex education in public schools stems from the fact that there is no clear, generally shared set of social values about sex in American society that can become the basis of a sex education course for teens. Perhaps the emerging effort to convince teens to say no to sex, as they were earlier urged to do with drugs, may provide such a basis.

Sooner or later, however, adolescents will want to know why they should say no. Values such as self-respect, fidelity, responsibility, self-discipline, and respect for others will need to be voiced. Perhaps older, biblical values such as sex within marriage, as God intended, can find a new hearing. Christians will then have an opportunity to participate in building a new moral consensus on sexuality in our society. That will be a significant gift not only to children of the future, but the entire society as well.

Beginning to Begin

During the Nixon administration when the press had gotten especially adept at pointing out discrepancies between administration policy and practice, Attorney General John Mitchell gave the press some advice. "Watch what we do, not what we say," he said. He implied that what was said really was not important, only the actions taken.

The Attorney General may have been a competent lawyer (before his prison term), but he did not know how to teach moral values. "Do what I say, not what I do" will not work in moral education. Life and lip must both agree.

Sexual education, as with moral education of any kind, begins at home. Parents are the primary means of the transmission of moral values to children, followed by teachers, church youth workers, Sunday school teachers, and other respected authorities. To the extent to which parents, religious teachers, and others exhibit an honesty and consistency between their professed values and their lives, they make it possible for children to identify and adopt those same values.

This, then, is where we Christian parents must begin: by being committed to speaking and living, clearly and consistently, our sexual values before our children. Premarital affairs (by single parents), extramarital affairs, or even unhealthy, disrespectful attitudes toward sex don't just hurt *us*—they hurt our children.

Once we are firmly committed to this understanding, we can begin the long process of building a new moral consensus on sex in our society, one that protects children and enriches childhood. We must speak out in support of sexual restraint. We must speak to public school officials, television executives, pornographers, and to anyone else who will listen.

What about those children whose parents do not understand or care about this threat to their children? We must also speak out for them. Who else will care enough to help present to these children their best hope for truly healthy, fulfilling marriages and families?

A few years ago, a television commercial urged us taking blood pressure medication, "if not for you, then for someone you love." If we love children *we must call our society to realize the awful price* that our children are paying for the sexual revolution.

Perhaps as our society continues to be alarmed at the sexual abuse and exploitation of children and the tragic consequences of teenage sexual activity, there will be an openness once again to rediscover the wisdom and health in the biblical teachings about sex. It is time to lead the fight for a third sexual revolution, if not for ourselves, then for the children we love.

FOUR

The Loss
of Family Stability

Junior high school students call it their worst fear, worse than war or death[1]; young people experience terrible nightmares over it. This fear, this lurking nightmare, is divorce. When parents divorce, children are immediately plunged into crisis. All sorts of confusing emotions, disturbing questions, and impossible choices suddenly confront them. "Who will take care of me now? What if Mommy leaves, too?" "What did I do to cause Mom to leave? Doesn't she love me anymore?" "I can't make up my mind which one to live with. It's not fair!"

Divorce turns a child's stable, secure, and friendly world upside down. Optimism turns to fear, happiness turns to anger, and carefree innocence turns to guilt.

Today over 1 million marriages end in divorce every year. Many children are losing that "intimate and protective environment providing nurture and care," stability and security, which a family provides.[2] For these children, their worst fears are coming true.

One of my favorite stories that I read to my sons when they were young was of a newly hatched baby bird. When he emerged from his egg, his mother had left the nest to find a worm to feed him. Finding himself alone, his first question was "Where is my mother?" and off he went to find her. The boys and I always laughed together as the little bird first asked a kitten, then a hen, a dog, a cow, a boat, and even a steam shovel, "Are *you* my mother?" At last, the story ends happily when he finds her.[3]

The story is so appealing to children because they know, perhaps instinctively, that everyone has a mother, but not just any mother will do! Each child has a mother that is just right for him or her. She matches; she fits.

Can the same be said of the family? Is there a family that is right for every child? Is it the traditional, two-parent family consisting of a father who goes off to work and a mother who stays home to care for the children? If so, there are few such families around anymore. This traditional family model comprises just 15 percent of all families in the United States today.

Between 1960 and 1985 the divorce rate approximately doubled. This fact, coupled with the significant rate of remarriage among divorced parents, created a number of new family forms in which many children now live. The most common are single-parent families, blended families, and joint custody families.

The steady increase in divorce in recent decades contributed significantly to a steady increase in single-parent families. About one in five children today lives in a single-parent family.[4] In the great majority of these families, the single parent is the mother.

Blended families are not new, of course. They were around even before Henry Fonda's comic struggle in the movie *Yours, Mine and Ours*. Again, however, higher divorce and remarriage rates in recent years have resulted in many more families consisting of "his kids, her kids, and our kids."

Blended families often present young children with adaptive challenges and considerable stress. Not only must a child adapt to a new parent ("Can I love my new Daddy and still love my old one, too?") but also to new siblings.

In joint custody families, both parents live separately and share custody of their minor children. When angry and often hostile parents can make it work, this arrangement helps make the best of a bad situation. The children involved retain regular contact with both parents and are not forced to choose which parent to live with. Some semblance of family stability is maintained. Currently, joint custody is permitted in thirty-two states.

Traditional families, single-parent families, joint custody families, blended families, and others are among the dizzying and growing variety of alternative forms of the family in America today. It is not unusual for a child to live in three or four of these types of families before reaching maturity.

Current trends suggest that approximately one in three children born in the 1980s will live in some form of stepfamily before reaching the age of eighteen. About 70 percent of these children will spend at least a part of their childhood or adolescence in a single-parent household.[5]

What kind of family is just right for a child? In most cases two parents still provide the most continuous, stable environment of love and care for the children. Why two parents? Ask any frazzled single mom (or dad) who comes home to a preschooler after a hard day at work. God gave children two parents for many reasons. One reason was, no doubt, that the time and energy needed by young children often is more than one parent can provide. Sometimes one needs to call in reinforcements and the other parent takes over.

Single-parent families face special challenges, and those single parents need and deserve all the help and encouragement their friends can provide. Despite the increase in joint custody arrangements and some willingness by courts to grant custody to fathers, the great majority of single-parent families are headed by women.

Even young children, however, become attached to their fathers. This attachment is normal, healthy, and good. It is important to a young child's healthy emotional growth and development that they learn to relate to adult males in a friendly, positive way.[6] Fathers usually fill this role for both girls and boys.

If the father is absent because of divorce, other adult males can help fill the child's need for companionship and modeling.[7] Here is a ready-made ministry that any Christian adult male, single or married, with or without children, can offer a young boy or girl in a single-parent home. No more qualifications are needed than to be yourself and be a friend.

Recent studies have shown that children in single-parent

families, especially those headed by women, are at risk. They are more likely to have a greater arrest rate and more academic and disciplinary problems in school. They are more likely than their peers who live with both parents to run away from home. This holds true regardless of race or income.[8]

There seems to be some correlation between being raised in a single-parent family and criminal tendencies, especially for boys.[9] Factors such as stable, consistent affection and consistent discipline from the single parent are more important to the child than simply having or not having both parents in the home, however.

Boys are especially at risk for problems caused by divorce. They are generally less well behaved and score lower on academic tests than boys who live with both parents. One researcher speculated that the effect of divorce on. boys was compounded by the fact that children do better with parents of the same sex, but in the great majority of cases, custody rights go to the mother.[10]

Why two parents? Children naturally want to keep both parents around them, loving them. They know that, in a real sense, they are made from both parents. If one parent leaves the family and is perceived to be some sort of scoundrel, the child, too, must be at least part scoundrel.[11] It is important for children to be able to believe in *both* parents to be able to grow up believing in themselves.[12]

God established the family and gave children two parents. He could have chosen differently; obviously, He felt two parents were best for children. Historically and experientially, the wisdom of the Creator in this regard has been proven over and over again.

What Makes a Family Just Right?

Robert Frost once described a family as "somewhere, when you have to go there, they have to take you in." His description is simple but insightful. It points to the most basic element of what makes a family just right to a child (even more than having both parents in the home). This basic element is a stable, secure, enduring relationship of love.

Children teach us how important stability and stable relationships are to them. What parent hasn't groaned inwardly (or rebelled outwardly) at reading the same book to a preschool child for the fourth night in a row? Breaking in a new babysitter was a major crisis at our house. Suddenly, my outgoing independent kindergartner became a tearful and clinging little boy. He already had two favorite, well-known, well-worn babysitters and willingly accepted no substitutes!

Those familiar, predictable bedtime stories which he knew as well as I (don't even try to skip a page!) represent stability, predictability, and security in a new and confusing world. With his favorite babysitter, he didn't have to wonder and worry about whether he would be well cared for and happy while we were gone. Previous experiences had answered those questions.

Harvard psychiatrist Armand Nicholi points out the devastation of a child by the loss of a parent in divorce and the threat to the ongoing relationship of love between the child and the parent who leaves.

> If we know anything about normal human development, it is that it rests heavily on a close, warm, sustained relationship with both parents. And if people with severe, emotional non-organic disorders have anything in common, it's that they have experienced, sometime in their childhood, an absence of an accessible parent because of death, divorce or a time consuming job. [13]

Again and again, research has shown the importance of stable, secure relationships of love to the emotional health of children. [14] Out of these relationships, where a child can count on his family to always "take him in," in Frost's words, he or she develops the ability to trust others and to trust in their love. He or she is then able to love others and let them love him or her (not fearing the loss of that love). Feeling loved and lovable contributes much to a child's sense of self-esteem and competence.

On the other hand, nearly all children of divorce suffer some emotional insecurity. They have seen one parent leave their home, which they often interpret as rejection, and only one parent is left. The child's most terrifying fear is abandonment.[15]

"I live with Mommy now. We are divorced from Daddy," said a little four-year-old girl. In her words is a sense of both pain and loss. Of course parents do not "divorce" their children, but when one parent leaves, the child often feels as if that is exactly what happened.

Child psychologist Lee Salk calls the trauma of divorce for children second only to death. "Children feel a deep sense of loss and feel they are suddenly vulnerable to forces beyond their control." For them, divorce means the collapse of their secure, protective family structure. Suddenly, they feel alone and frightened.[16]

Another common problem experienced by children of divorce is what David Elkind calls a "free-floating anxiety." The children are restless and irritable, often unable to concentrate on schoolwork. Sometimes they are not even aware of the cause of their trouble. The loss and instability caused by divorce is extremely stressful to children, even years after their parents' divorce.[17]

Stress, worry, fear, and anger all may combine to catch a child in that most unchildlike of conditions, depression. Some children become so depressed that they fantasize suicide. Suicide, they feel, may be the only way to bring their parents back together again.[18]

Pam, who was twelve when her parents divorced, perked up whenever her father came to visit her after the divorce. Each time she hoped and tried to believe he would tell her that her parents were getting back together again. Finally, she realized it would not happen and became terribly angry and depressed.

The economics of divorce often create great pain and instability for children, also. No-fault divorce has been an economic disaster for women and children. Studies show that the average divorce decree decreases the standard of living of the woman by 73 percent (while that of the husband increases by 43 percent).[19]

In 1959 about one in four poor families was headed by a female. By 1982 nearly one in two poor families was headed by a female.[20] During this same period the divorce rate doubled. These statistics underscore the economic effect of divorce on women and their dependent children. It has thrown many of them into poverty.

The sense of vulnerability, loss, and instability for the children involved is not hard to understand. Mom is no longer at home with them and they may be forced into day care. Such necessities as medical care, to say nothing of some of childhood's small luxuries, are now beyond reach.

Not all children experience divorce in the same way or with the same intensity. Judson Swihart and Steve Brigham, family counselors, cite a study of children of divorce that demonstrates these different outcomes. Approximately one-third of the children came through the divorce successfully: They ended up with positive self-images and had good outlooks on life. Another third "muddled through," having quite a few problems and some successes. The rest, the authors say, "never recovered from the trauma and hence continued hurt and injured, always hoping and wishing that things could go back as they were."[21]

What about those children who made it through a divorce successfully? Were they happier after the split? Were they glad to be relieved of their parents' constant fighting? Was the divorce good for them?

Pam knew her parents fought a lot. From the time she was eight until their divorce when she was twelve, they seemed to fight constantly. But when her mom told her that her dad had left and a divorce was planned, it did not hurt any less. She woke up in a sweat from a terrible nightmare where she dreamed she was separated from both her parents. Psychiatrist Archibald Hart, himself a child of divorce, warns that no matter how resilient or emotionally healthy a child seems, it is safe to assume "that the divorce will have some damaging effect on him or her."[22]

Some parents contemplating divorce today still ask the question, "Should we stay together for the good of the children?" A recent psychological study of the effects of divorce on adolescents offers an answer. The study indicates that, from the perspective of the good of the child, there is only one argument in favor of divorce: the reduction of the atmosphere of family conflict in which the child must live.[23]

When two people are caught up in the anger and struggle of a divorce, they necessarily work hard to protect themselves from all the pain. The needs of young children can be overlooked. The intense anger and resentment often present in a divorce creates an intense fear in the child: "The younger the child, the more damaging the climate of anger can be."[24]

Psychologists Nicholas Long and Rex Forehand compared the social and academic adjustment of twenty adolescents whose parents were recently divorced and twenty whose parents stayed together. Their research did not concern itself with long-term effects of divorce or with questions of biblical faith and practice. The best they could say for divorce was that if it reduced the family conflict, it might be plausible, but otherwise it is "a horrible option."[25]

It is well known that children willingly put up with great tension in the family (and even physical and emotional abuse) rather than see their parents divorce. More often it is the parents who seek relief from family tensions through divorce.

On the other hand, less than one child in ten experiences any "relief" from his parents' divorce. He or she is no happier after the divorce and his or her psychological health may not improve significantly.[26] Studies indicate that over one-third of children of divorce are still depressed by the break-up of their family five years later.[27]

Something that needs to be said and said clearly is that divorce is almost always harmful to a dependent child (except perhaps in cases of extreme abuse). The cords of love and trust between parent and child are broken and the child is thrown (at least as he or she feels it) out of a secure, protective, welcoming world into a threatening, unpredictable, and unreliable one. Every way they look at it, children lose.

Children between the ages of five and eight years old seem most vulnerable to the losses caused by divorce. They are old enough to understand what is happening to their families but too young to deal with it well. At this age they tend to feel guilty for causing their parents' divorce. The result can be lowered self-esteem, anger, depression, and, in extreme cases, suicidal fantasies.[28]

There is never a "best time" to get a divorce when children are involved. Those estranged spouses who in the past stayed together and endured the pain for the good of the children take on almost heroic stature today. They have almost all disappeared now and are rapidly being replaced by spouses who see divorce as the key to their own happiness and self-fulfillment. Their children are just unfortunate victims who will have to make the best of whatever arrangements result.

Were they asked, their children would echo the wise counsel of Archibald Hart:

> . . . my experience as a psycho-therapist and the research available to us on the outcome of divorce has led me to believe that, when it is at all possible, saving the existing marriage is infinitely preferable to divorcing; this course of action is far more likely to lead to a fulfilling and satisfying life for all the parties concerned.[29]

This applies doubly, Hart might have added, to children.

There remain those children who do come through divorce reasonably healthy emotionally. They are the happy exceptions to the gloomy rule. These exceptions happen most probably because, even in the midst of their own pain and loss, the parents managed to maintain for their children a measure of stability and love.

"He explained their divorce and also his love for me," Pam

said of her father. "I went to bed that night feeling totally different than most kids do when their parents get divorced." Though her parents were living apart, she knew they both still loved her. Nothing could, or would, ever change that.

Parents do not divorce their children, but sometimes it sure seems that way! Those parents who can rise above their pain to assure their children that they are and always will be loved by both parents can still provide much of the stability of environment and relationship (the two go together in a child's mind) that their children need and desire.

Sometimes, tragically, parents will have to do this in the midst of a divorce. Others, perhaps, can rediscover the willingness to stay together and make it work for their children's sake. They will struggle, suffer, and sacrifice on behalf of their children.

Those who do this will give their children a priceless gift: the experience of the unconditional, unbreakable love of God Himself. That love, experienced through their parents' love, can be trusted. It will always be there for their children. Whenever the child has to go there it will always take him in. That experience of God's love through the family will prepare that child for his or her life's greatest relationship: loving and trusting God.

Parents, God, and Divorce

God hates divorce. Marriage vows are meant to be permanent and unbreakable, reflecting the permanence of God's vow of love for His people. Divorce is a denial by the spouses of both their marriage vows and the nature of God's vows. Although the biblical writers recognized the legitimacy of divorce for infidelity, God Himself is never unfaithful. He keeps His vows! He does not divorce His people.

The experience of divorce, then, may warp a child's understanding of God and of His relationship to His people. The Psalmist's affirmation that when his father and mother reject him, God will take him in, is an adult response. Children may feel the opposite: If Mom or Dad reject me, surely God will also.

Most often today divorce means that the father leaves the home. If the children are young when he leaves, they may grow up lacking a true father figure. As a result, they may have little understanding of what a father is like, and what God their Heavenly Father is like.

Our culture has been slow to acknowledge the feminine and nurturing aspects of God's nature portrayed in the Bible. Although there is a real sense in which God is a mother, predominately, He is revealed in the Bible as a father. A child's earliest and most direct understanding of what God the Father is like results from this relationship with the parents, especially his or her father.

Nowhere is this more vividly seen than in the life of the great Reformer, Martin Luther. Luther's father, Hans, was a cold, harsh, and an authoritarian man. In young Martin's family, his father's stern presence and the anticipation of his punishment seem to have pervaded the family atmosphere. Hans Luther became the embodiment of a cold, jealous God to his young son Martin.[30]

Growing up with this man as his earthly image of God, young Martin's spiritual understanding of God was seriously warped. Martin could never please his father, it seemed. His self-esteem suffered. He could never feel loved or accepted by either his father or by God.

Young Luther, although he became a priest, transferred his relationship with his father to his relationship to God. Luther "had an overwhelming sense of the majesty and wrath of God."[31] He wrestled with the fear that he was a child of destruction, never able to be redeemed.

As he could never please his father or feel loved and accepted by him, Luther felt full of self-hate and guilt when he thought about God. He was, as one observer put it, "sickened by the idea that God is just," because if so, it meant he was doomed.[32] To be justified before this God became "his stumbling block as a believer and his obsession as a man and a theologian."[33]

Only after much pain and struggle, God's grace broke through to him as he read Paul's Epistle to the Romans. There he found the answer he longed for: "The just shall live by faith."[34] God's forgiveness is given freely, in love, to all who trust Him. It need not, and cannot be earned. When he realized this, Luther was finally set free to feel loved and accepted by God. At last he was "able to forgive God for being a father," like his own.[35]

Martin Luther's experience was especially dramatic, perhaps, but essentially similar to that of children born before and since. Their deepest understanding of God and the basis of their early relationship with God grow out of their family experiences. How does divorce affect those understandings and relationships?

Luther came close to rejecting his faith altogether, and such may be the case of some children of divorce. Children of Christian parents may rightly ask why the spiritual resources of the Christian faith cannot help their parents hold the family together. Is faith of no significance? Is God to blame?

In their anger and disillusionment over their parents' divorce, some children reject their parents' spiritual values. Children from the age of ten into their teens are especially vulnerable to this rejection since their major emotion at divorce is often anger. Developmentally they are at the stage in life when they are beginning to develop a faith of their own. Anger over the break-up of their family can lead to anger at the Christian faith.

Undermining the growing faith of a young child, or the basis of later faith (in the case of children raised in non-Christian families), is arguably the single most serious consequence of divorce for children. The future faith of many children is at risk in the divorce epidemic of today.

Love and security (stability) within relationships are at the heart of the spiritual struggles of children of divorce.[36] The consistent, ongoing love of both parents for each other and for their child becomes a direct expression and experience of God's faithful, consistent love for them. If Mom or Dad, whom I can see, cannot be counted on to be there for me, or if, all of a sudden, one or both of them abandon me, how can I expect more from God, whom I cannot see? That is a child's spiritual dilemma.

Sometimes divorce makes a young child's struggle to feel loved and accepted by God too painful. The way to stop the pain is to stop trying, as Luther nearly did. At least the pain of failure stops.

Recent research shows that children of divorce suffer from a poorer self-image than children from intact families.[37] This feeling of unworthiness is often born of the rejection of divorce and compounded by the guilt of feeling somehow responsible for it (common especially to children in the early elementary years). This poor self-image and heavy burden of guilt may be too much for a young conscience to bear: It is too much to expect God to love me and forgive me with this on my record!

There is a further consequence of divorce for children growing up within the Christian community. Divorce often makes it more difficult for children to worship God. True worship is respect, if not real love.

It will not be so easy for a child to join the rest of the congregation in praising God for His love and faithfulness while bearing the scars of rejection and abandonment, fear and guilt. Absolute, unquestioning trust—the heart of a child's faith—Jesus commended as a model for all adults. Will a child whose father has left his or her family be so ready to trust the Heavenly Father? Certainly God can and does heal and overcome these wounds, as He did for Martin Luther. But who wants to be responsible for inflicting them?

Undermining the faith of a child is deadly serious business. Jesus said of such a person that "it would be better for him to have a large millstone hung around his neck and to be drowned in the depths of the sea" than to undermine a child's faith.[38] Parents getting divorced may be doing just that.

Since it is most often the father who leaves the home, young boys probably suffer the most spiritually (and emotionally) from divorce. They lose the everyday love and care of one who represents God's fatherly love and care. They also lose a model of the man of God that they could one day become, a man who, though strong and independent, kneels before God and humbly trusts in His care.

Hosea the prophet was called by God to marry Gomer the prostitute. Hosea obeyed and was a loving, faithful husband. But Gomer was not faithful and it hurt Hosea deeply. Yet Hosea did not divorce Gomer. Likewise, God does not divorce His people.

FIVE

The Loss of Parenting: The Dilemma of Day Care

For fifty-eight hours in the fall of 1987 the eyes of the world were fixed on a little girl in a little town in Texas. Hourly news reports told of the scores of volunteers racing to rescue little Jessica McClure.

Nineteen-month-old Jessica had fallen down an old dry well one day while attending an unlicensed (illegal) family day-care program near her home. Despite the danger, she was lucky. She survived.

There was no such happy ending in Miami, Florida. There a single mother worked all day to support her two sons, ages three and four. She did not make enough to pay the rent and day care. One day, when there were not any friends or relatives who could look after the boys, she left them alone in the house and went to work. It was that or lose her job. Sometime during the day the boys crawled into the clothes dryer to play. It started up; they tumbled and burned to death.

Since 1970 the rate of employment outside the home for married women with children under six has risen from 30 to 50 percent.[1] Most of these children, an estimated 9 million, need some form of day care.

Needing it and finding it, however, are two different things. By the most optimistic estimates, there are only enough licensed day-care centers to accommodate 25 percent of the young children who need day care.

T. Berry Brazelton, professor of pediatrics at Harvard Medical

School, estimates that there are only enough good quality day-care centers for 10 percent of the children needing care. Day care, it seems, is "hard to find, difficult to afford, and often of distressingly low quality."[2]

State licensed and supervised day-care facilities might be expected to provide at least reasonable quality day care. But licensing is no guarantee. Since 1980 thirty-three states have lowered their licensing standards for day care and reduced their enforcement of the standards that remain. Only three states, Kansas, Massachusetts, and Maryland, require a ratio of at least one adult to every three infants in day care, the highest ratio most experts agree to be desirable for good quality care.

It is not uncommon to find day-care centers with adult to infant ratios of one to six or even one to eight. In these situations the care received by the babies can only be minimal at best. Today approximately one of every two working mothers returns to work before her baby's first birthday. Infant day care, which is the most demanding and expensive, is often stretched beyond safe limits.

Dr. Brazelton tells of a four-month-old baby who was accepted at the day-care center where his three-year-old brother attended every day. Within two weeks his mother noticed the change: The baby grew pale and began to eat poorly, and he seemed unusually sensitive to loud noises. He was overwhelmed by his parents' attempts to play with him each evening.

The pediatrician checked him thoroughly and found no physical problems. There was one other clue, however. The baby had been losing weight and "failing to thrive," as the doctor called it. His mother knew something was wrong at the day-care center and she went to investigate, determined to find the problem.

What she found in the center's infant room was one overworked, underpaid woman who had only enough time and energy to hurriedly feed and infrequently change all the infants in her care. She did her best, but most of the day the babies were left in their cribs without the personal interaction and stimulation infants need to develop normally. The baby missed the enthusiastic play and cuddling he had received at home those first four months. He became withdrawn and depressed.

Dr. Brazelton tells this story to illustrate some of the problems and dangers to children (not just infants) of day care.[3] His is one of a growing number of voices raising serious questions about the future of those 9 million young children.

Yale psychologist Edward Zigler, one of the developers of Project Head Start, calls trying to find good quality day care "a cosmic crapshoot." Finding good day care is often simply a matter of luck. And, he says, "There's a lot of mediocre child care out there and some absolutely horrible day care."[4]

Buying day care is after all, Zigler continues, "buying an environment that determines, in large part, the development" of young children. Parents must be aware that the "physical and mental development of millions of children are being compromised" by inadequate and damaging day care.[5]

There are alternatives to licensed day-care centers, of course. One is home care, where your child is cared for, usually in your home, by a sitter or relative. About 30 percent of children requiring day care are in home care. Another 35 to 40 percent are in family day care, where the child is cared for by another mother in her home usually along with her own children.

Sometimes these can be excellent arrangements, depending on the individual caregiver and the situation involved. My wife provided family day care for a preschool girl each weekday morning for two years while our youngest son was also a preschooler.

But each situation and caregiver must be examined carefully. Some family day care is licensed and some, like that which almost cost Jessica McClure her life, is not. Too many children, especially young ones, can overburden even the best-intentioned mother. The tragedies mount: a twenty-month-old boy who drowned in a backyard pool of a sitter supervising too many children, two preschoolers who died in a fire in Brooklyn when the sitter could not save all the children, and so on.

Family day care, if carefully chosen, offers some advantages over day-care centers, especially if the caregiver is a mother herself. She can be a real mother-substitute for a child. In family day care, turnover of caregivers—a real problem in many day-care centers—will likely be lower.

Many times the most comfortable situation for the child is to be cared for in his or her own home by a sitter or relative (home care). There is something special about being in your own home, playing with your own toys. Remember, check the quality of supervision, the attitude and motivation of the caregiver, and the caregiver's references.[6]

Of course, the quality of even licensed facilities is unpredictable at best. Reasons are not hard to find. Day-care workers rank in the lowest 10 percent of all American wage earners (the average annual wage is $9000). Almost 60 percent of day-care workers earn poverty-level wages or less. Such low wages do not normally attract the highly trained professionals whom parents expect to provide quality day care for their infants and children.

Furthermore, such low wages could not be expected to hold even those good people who might take a day-care position. Undertrained and underpaid, they are likely to leave at the first offer of a good paying job. In fact, about 40 percent of child-care workers are replaced each year. This high turnover rate of day-care workers (which is exactly the opposite of one criterion of quality day care) is compounded by the fact that many parents change their child's day-care arrangements annually, whether for reasons of cost, convenience, or quality.[7]

The results of these frequent changes in caregivers is that day care has become a high risk game of "Whom can you trust?" for many children. The answer keeps coming up "No one."

Young children need continuity in relationships with those who provide their earliest and primary care. As early as one month of age, they come to love and depend on the one or two people who are their primary caregivers. The security and continuity of these early relationships enable an infant to learn to love, because he or she is loved, and to trust those whose love he or she returns.

It is not just adults who experience the pain of unrequited love. If an infant or young child has too many caregivers (more than a couple) during the first year or two of life, he or she cannot form the secure and lasting bonds of love and attachment needed for emotional and spiritual health. Just when the child begins to love and trust the caregiver at day care, it seems, the caregiver disappears. The child feels rejected, and he or she has to start all over again.

Over two or three years in day care, this cycle may repeat itself. Finally, the disappointment and pain of each loss is too great. The damage is done. The child loses some, perhaps much, of his or her capacity to love and trust others deeply and intimately. Some of the willingness to commit to others is lost—whether friends, a future spouse, or God. He or she may also become more self-centered and attracted to material objects, showing less emotional attachment to people.[8]

Children are *not* somehow more flexible than adults. If anything, they are less flexible. They thrive on stability, continuity, and routine, as we have seen. Change is often a cause of stress in a young child's life. Repeated changes in caregivers for children under three can be stressful and even damaging. Yet that is exactly what is happening to many children in day care today.[9]

It is important to maintain the same primary caregivers during a child's first three years, if at all possible. Who is better than a child's parents to maintain that crucial continuity of love and care?

For many parents, especially low-income families and single parents (usually mothers), finding good quality day care is only part of the problem. Paying for it is even more difficult. The best day care can cost $100 per week or more. Infant day care is the most demanding and expensive. It is no surprise that finding good, affordable day care has become "the most wrenching personal problem facing millions of American families."[10]

The search for good quality, affordable day care is most wrenching and stressful for the 15 percent of all American households headed by women. These single women (90 percent of all single parents are women) almost always have to work to support themselves and their children. They earn only about 70 percent of what men earn for comparable work, and less than one-third receive child support.[11]

Their problem with day care is obvious: More than 50 percent of these families have incomes below the poverty level. For one in four children overall or one in every two black children, living in a single-parent home is actually a euphemism for poverty.

For some of these women the choice is literally survival or day care. One woman put it simply: "If I don't have to pay the baby sitter, I can survive." The result of having to make this choice is often leaving a young child unsupervised, as that mother of two preschoolers in Miami did. "I couldn't have afforded a baby sitter. So we had, out of necessity, to work it out to where I knew the kids would be safe," one single mother said.[12]

When no day care of any kind is affordable, it is no wonder a mother is worried to death at letting her five year old come home to an empty house daily after school.[13] But too much wasted time at work worrying, too much time on the phone checking up on the child, and too much sick leave to care for sick children and you lose your job.

Although the lack of affordable day care, and the risks that it poses to children are most burdensome for single mothers and low-income families, even middle-income families struggle with the costs. Edward Zigler sees another danger to children: the development of a two-tier day-care system.

Affluent families are able to buy into the first tier of a limited amount of high-quality, expensive day care. The rest will have "to accept mediocre or even dangerous care for their children." Zigler continues:

> We can not have a society in which some children at 3 weeks of age are sent into a child care system that helps their development while another group is put into a system that is damaging.[14]

Children in this second tier, whose families cannot afford good quality day care, are often already at risk. They are already vulnerable because they come from single-parent homes or from families with low incomes, significant deprivation, and inadequate health care. Poor quality day care puts them at even greater risk.

It does not take a lot of difficult analysis to see the long-range dangers to our future society posed by this "hodge podge, jumbled, patchwork" day-care system. Christians, especially, who share their Lord's love for children and His concern for the weak and vulnerable know they cannot be indifferent.

In fact, indifference to the problems and challenges day care poses to children and their families probably will not be possible much longer. By 1995, in less than a decade, it is estimated that 15 million preschoolers will have mothers who work outside the home. A whole generation will require day care!

Assuming that by then affordable, good quality day care is available to every child who needs it (a big assumption), what effect will that have on those millions of young children? What are the effects on a preschool child of spending twenty to forty hours (or more) each week in day care?

Child development experts are not in general agreement on the answer to that question. One reason may be that widespread day care of children under the age of three is still relatively new. The impact may not be clear until a couple of generations of children can be studied.

Widespread use of day care, especially infant care, would have been inconceivable a generation ago. In the 1950s, day care was generally perceived as harmful to children, based largely on the work of the English psychologist John Bowlby. Americans believed that mothers should be at home caring for their children. Poor and single mothers (populations that highly overlap) might be forced to use day care. For middle-class families, however, the thought of putting their children in day care was as shocking as if the families on "Leave it to Beaver" and "Father Knows Best" did it.

By the 1970s, however, social forces were at work to change all this. The impact of the individual rights movements—civil rights, women's rights, gay rights, and others—had been felt throughout the country. Feminism had firmly established that women had a right and, in the face of a growing divorce rate, a real need for a career, with all the fulfillment and financial independence it brings. The great movement of women of childbearing age into the workforce began in earnest. [15]

The shift in acceptance of day care took place largely within the span of one generation. What had been unacceptable gradually became socially acceptable. If women were going to have careers, day care was necessary.

A number of social trends began to converge on the American family at this time: a growing divorce rate, the increase in mothers working outside the home, and the increasing shift of the responsibility of the care of young children to individuals and agencies other than parents. It is arguable that the most striking of these trends, in terms of significance for young children, was the shift toward day care. This move has robbed millions of young children of the daily care of their parents (usually their mothers) during their critical, formative early years.

As *Time* observed wryly, the opinions of experts on child rearing are "no less subject to fashion than the length of hemlines."[16] In 1968, when day care was still largely out of favor with middle-class America, Benjamin Spock labeled infant day care a "baby farm" that offered no benefits to infants. Day-care centers simply were too crowded to offer infants the undivided attention and affections they needed, he felt.[17]

By 1985, however, infant day care had become a growth industry and much in demand. That year the latest revision of Spock's classic book, *Baby and Child Care*, contained none of his earlier harsh criticism of infant day care (though a careful reading indicates he still has serious reservations).[18]

One major factor in this acceptance of day care for young children and infants was a study released in 1978 by Pennsylvania State University psychologist Jay Belsky. His research was widely influential in persuading parents and others of the advantages day care offers in promoting the social and intellectual development of children.

Indeed, many parents see earlier social and intellectual development as a big plus in favor of day-care centers. One mother was pleased that her child had learned so much from playing with other children in a day-care center: "He learned how to share and how limits get set. And he has a lot of activities he never had at home, like painting and fingerpainting."[19]

A generation or two ago, young children learned these same social and intellectual skills at home. Larger families and cousins nearby to play with provided plenty of opportunities to learn "how to share and how limits get set." A little input from Mom, Grandma, or an aunt helped promote creativity and intellectual stimulation. Today, however, falling birth rates, high family mobility, and the increase in mothers working outside the home have made it more difficult for children to develop these social and intellectual skills at home.

Music, arts and crafts, stories, and other learning experiences are what please these parents most about their child's day-care center. Recent studies confirm that many parents place their children in day-care centers (instead of in the home of a mother who is caring for them in addition to her own children) because they want their children to benefit from the programs and activities that day-care centers offer.

Any day-care arrangement will not provide those benefits. Some, such as the one Dr. Brazelton told of, can be demanding on day-care workers. In some situations infants probably *are* neglected and *do* become depressed. Unlicensed family day care in an overworked mother's home can result in children hurt or killed (as in the Miami tragedy) or stuck in front of the television all day. These "horror stories" do not characterize all, perhaps not even most, day-care arrangements. But they do happen. Everyone agrees *that* kind of day care is harmful.

On the other hand, experts tell us good quality day care can be beneficial to young children.[20] Key factors have to do with the quality of the care and the age of the child upon entering day care.

What *is* good quality day care? The criteria on which most experts agree are the following: a state-licensed facility, a staff trained in child development or early childhood education, low staff turnover, and a low staff-to-child ratio (from one adult to every three children to one to five, depending on the ages of the children). [21]

As we have seen, day care that meets these standards is in short supply and expensive. Licensed day-care centers can accommodate only 25 percent of day-care needs at best. They are often plagued by high staff turnover and dangerously high numbers of children for each adult caregiver. Home care and family care *can* be beneficial, but their quality is unpredictable. Each situation must be evaluated individually and carefully.

Suppose you do find a day-care center where it seems your young child will have continuity of care. Or you put your child in a family day-care situation with another mother. Can you relax now, assured that your child will benefit from these secure and stable attachments?

The answer is perhaps. The larger question is with whom will your child develop his or her earliest, most formative attachments and bonds? Who will shape your child's personality and attitude toward life during those critical early years?

It is generally accepted that a child's experiences with his or her parents or other primary caregivers during the first three years play a major role in shaping personality and general outlook on life. As we have seen, those earliest relationships develop in a child a sense of trust and security in the world so that he or she can be a trusting, secure individual, not always cool and suspicious or emotionally distant. Such a child, who knows he or she is loved and valued, will more easily grow to be a generally happy, optimistic individual.

Day-care centers can be exciting places, especially for parents! Fingerpainting and blocks are available to toddlers; musical instruments are offered to two year olds. Some centers use flash cards to develop early academic skills.

But all this intellectual stimulation will be largely wasted unless these children develop secure bonds of love to their parents and a sense of being loved and worthwhile themselves. Then they can focus their efforts on learning. Healthy emotional development is the foundation on which intellectual development is built. Unfortunately, it does not work the other way around. A young child's development is clearly a case of "first things first."

Without that secure foundation, unresolved emotional learning tasks slow down and even block intellectual development. By making it more difficult for young children to form secure bonds of love with either of their parents (when they are put in day care at eight weeks or four months) or with day-care workers (who keep leaving), we run the risk of robbing these children both emotionally *and* intellectually.

Dr. Belsky,whose 1978 study provided support for the widespread acceptance of day care a decade ago, is raising some serious questions about it now. He is especially concerned about the effect of day care on infants and toddlers (under eighteen months of age) who are left in day-care centers twenty hours or more each week.

Belsky's recent studies led him to warn that children who are removed from their mother's care while under the age of one are more likely to be emotionally insecure and less attached to their mother. He told the *Wall Street Journal* that he now believes that infant day care can damage a young child's "sense of trust, of security, of order in the world."[22] His findings are especially frightening in light of the fact that 50 percent of mothers who work outside the home return to work before their baby's first birthday.

By the time these infants enter kindergarten, having spent three or more years in day care, their emotional problems will be evident. They are likely to be aggressive and uncooperative in their behavior. Here is Belsky's advice: If a mother can stay home with her baby at least during the first year, she should do it. [23]

Belsky's finding of a weakened emotional bond between mother and child has been confirmed by other studies, even those whose authors seem less concerned about it. [24] Some others have sharply criticized his recommendations. They see no reason why such an intense emotional bond between a child and its mother is either necessary or desirable. A bond of love to someone else—just about anyone else—might serve as well, they say. [25]

This raises an even more serious question for Christian parents. Children do not just catch colds in day care. It is inevitable that if they spend thirty, forty, or more hours each week in the care of someone else, growing dependent on and closely attached to that person, they will catch that person's attitudes and values.

What attitudes and values are being passed around at *your* neighborhood day-care center? If your child's attitudes and values are being formed during these first three years, whose attitudes are doing the forming? What Christian parent would willingly give up and give over to a largely unknown day-care worker or neighborhood mother the tremendous privilege and responsibility of shaping his child's deepest, most lasting attitudes and values? The answer to those questions exposes perhaps the most serious risk that day care represents: Who is raising our children, and how?

Two or three years is not a long time in the context of eternity, but it is long enough to lay the foundation of a child's life. An emotionally secure child who has learned during those years that he or she can trust in the parents' unconditional love and care has been given a most precious gift: the foundation for a natural, spontaneous response of love and trust for God, the Heavenly Father.

This child knows in his deepest being who he or she is, a child who is loved by his or her parents. Furthermore, if this child realizes the greatest love of all, the love of the Heavenly Father, this child can also love others.

"Love your neighbor as yourself," Jesus said.[26] Jesus knew that a healthy self-love is an absolute prerequisite for truly loving others. On the other hand, a child who is unattached to his or her parents, who is unsure of their love, will find it harder to love either self or others.

These are the risks, emotional and spiritual, that young children in day care are subjected to daily. Is this too dark a picture of the risks of day care? Are there ways to minimize those risks?

The risks to young children posed by day care are, at least potentially, serious. Experts disagree, as we have seen, but many echo the words of the prominent child psychologist who warned that the majority of children who spend forty hours per week in day-care centers will suffer permanent psychological damage.[27] And there will also be spiritual damage.

Reducing the risk of such harm to young children is dependent on three factors: the age of the child upon entering day care, the amount of time spent there, and, of course, the quality and continuity of care.

What is the age of least risk to start a child in day care? Or, to put it another way, when is the best time for a mother to return to work (or for parents who are sharing care of their infant to put him or her in day care)?

There is probably no totally risk-free age under three at which to start a child in day care. Most experts are coming to agree that children under the age of one, however, are the most vulnerable to the effects of being removed from the care of their parents.

A good rule to follow in deciding how long to care for your child at home is that "longer is better"; if possible keep them home up to the age of three. By then most young children are ready for and can benefit from a good preschool or nursery school program. Similarly, when deciding how many hours per week to put a child in day care, the best rule is "shorter is better," again, up to the age of three.[28]

It is going to take more than expert advice, however, to make it possible and probable that young children do stay in the care of their parents for that critical first year and even longer. It will take a new commitment on the part of adults, especially parents, to the welfare of their children.

Belsky said it well: "There are some risks out there for kids" in day care. "We have to decide which risks we are willing to take and which ones we are not."[29] Better yet, perhaps, would be the decision not to expose our children to such risks at all! That in itself would reflect a major change for the good in the attitude of adults toward the welfare of young children.

For those children whose parents have little choice about day care or whose parents ignore the risks, people who care about children will work for changes in the day-care system. Flexible working hours and paid sick leave (and sick days usable for self or children) will help single mothers substantially. Maternity and paternity leaves with partial pay and guaranteed return to work will help parents who want to care for their infants themselves.

"Our future as a productive nation depends upon our children. Our failure to invest in high quality child care endangers that future."[30] There are risks for kids in day care—risks of real physical, emotional, and spiritual loss.

Parents who bravely (or even fearfully) entrust their young children to day care are either pioneers taking necessary risks in pursuit of their dreams or are foolishly "flying blind," taking unacceptable risks with their children's futures. In either case their children are guinea pigs in a great social experiment. Only time will tell the full extent of their loss.

SIX

The Loss
of Care and Supervision:
Children in a
"Care-Less" Society

I n the mid and late 1970s, strange things began to happen in many cities and towns. Neighborhood elementary school buildings in which generations of children had been educated began to be sold and converted to other uses. School districts that had for years been used to straining their budgets to build schools, began to close them instead.

Organized programs of all kinds for elementary age children began to find their enrollment dropping. Sunday school attendance declined too. It did not take a lot of investigative work to figure out the reason for this. The birth rate had dropped; there were fewer children being born.

What happened to cause this decline in the number of young children? Why, in just a decade or two, had their numbers decreased so? There are multiple causes, including some related to the changes in the economic functions of families and children. But it is also clear that a significant change had taken place in the attitude of many adults toward children.

Sometime, somehow, many adults had decided to have fewer children, to spend less time with the children they did have, and to provide their children with less supervision than in previous generations. That change in attitude is now clear: Many adults simply "care less" for children today.

That attitude change really began in the period between World War I and World War II. Influential sociologists began to publish their understanding of the family as no longer child centered. Its purpose was no longer understood as primarily for the bearing and raising of children.

These experts pointed out that child bearing had become an economic liability to parents. They predicted that smaller families or even childless families would gradually replace large families. The extended family of three or even four generations living under one roof would gradually disappear. [1]

If we do not enter and maintain lasting marriage commitments as a primary means of providing a healthy, stable environment for child rearing, why *do* we get married? Primarily for companionship, sociologists answered. We marry primarily for our own self-fulfillment. [2] Children are not a central element in married life.

This change in our understanding of marriage fits nicely with the sensitivities of the "me generation" of the 1960s and 70s. Finding that "me" is true happiness, true self-fulfillment. And that self-fulfillment is, after all, the ultimate goal of life. Personal relationships also serve that same goal.

An important shift in our understanding of personal relationships (and that most personal relationship called marriage) has taken place. Relationships between people, even in marriage, have become almost totally self-directed and self-centered. They are supposed to be exclusively for my benefit, my growth, my convenience. One of the most "other-directed," "other-centered" goals of the marriage relationship, bearing and raising children, has clearly faded by comparison.

A real tension has been created between children and parents because children, too, almost by definition, are self-centered. As a result they can be demanding and inconvenient! They require parents to sacrifice some of their own personal goals and freedoms to provide their children with proper care and supervision.

Many adults have simply decided children are not worth those sacrifices. So couples are having fewer children and often providing less care and supervision for the ones they do have. Children are not so special anymore. And their parents are often acting more like children than adults!

A study presented to the National Council of Family Relations illustrates this change in attitude toward children. Researchers asked 600 couples who had been married up to six years (some with, some without children) to cite the advantages and disadvantages of having children. The research team found that couples today see fewer advantages and more disadvantages to having children than couples did just twenty years ago.[3]

American family lore celebrates those parents, some recent immigrants, some not, who worked long and hard and gladly gave up even simple luxuries their entire lives so that their children "would have it better than we did." These parents made a commitment to their children and their children's future. They sacrificed to honor that commitment and did so proudly. Their children were special!

Recent surveys illustrate how that attitude of willingness to sacrifice has eroded. The research team cited above found that the advantages of having children mentioned by parents a generation ago, such as "carrying on the family name, creating a sense of accomplishment" had been replaced by a greater focus on the disadvantages of children. Commonly mentioned were the disruption to individual lifestyle, the high cost of raising children, and the inconvenience to a wife's career.[4]

Changing attitudes toward marriage today send a similar message about the eroding commitment of adults to the bearing and raising of children. Birth control technology made it possible by the mid-1960s to separate successfully the personal companionship and fulfillment offered by marriage from the bearing and nurturing of children. It became not only possible but even popular to make the nurturing of children a secondary element in the marriage relationship.

Why has marriage, traditionally seen as a permanent union of a man and a woman, been so highly valued in the past apart from a commitment to biblical values? One compelling reason has been that a stable environment of two loving parents provided the best environment for raising children who could turn out to be healthy, productive adults.

On the other hand, one of the central arguments against divorce has been the terrible psychological pain inflicted on the children involved. In the face of these arguments, however, a high divorce rate continues unabated.

Deemphasizing the central place of children in marriage has undermined social pressure to maintain marriage vows and "to stay together for the good of the children." By overemphasizing a self-centered personal fulfillment view of marriage, we adults have made it much more acceptable to end a marriage which "isn't right for me," or "isn't fulfilling anymore," regardless of the needs of the children involved.

Faced with the grim facts about what divorce does to children, more adults than ever before have simply chosen to put their own "need for psychological well being" ahead of the needs of their children. The sacrifice, they have decided, is not worth it. Neil Postman draws a painful but accurate conclusion: "There has been a precipitous falling off in the commitment of adults to the nurturing of children."[5] We adults care less for children.

None Is Enough

America at the end of the twentieth century has become a care-less society regarding children. There is clearly a diminished willingness to bear, care for, and supervise young children. Rather than a precious gift from God and one's legacy to the future, children are often viewed as economic and professional liabilities.

Television shows such as "Eight Is Enough" or movies such as *Cheaper by the Dozen* seem like quaint artifacts from another era. Both the birth rate and family size have declined in recent decades. Some couples ponder child bearing and decide "none is enough!"

Among those who feel this way are couples who represent the newest socioeconomic phenomenon, DINKS. They are Dual Income couples with No Kids. Both partners have careers and have consciously decided not to have children. These are typical reasons they give:

> I didn't want to change my lifestyle. I don't want to have kids around me reasonably expecting to be part of the action. We have the flexibility to basically do what we want. We can vacation, do things our friends can afford.[6]

And talk about inconvenient! Children never get sick on weekends, when it's easier to care for them. They always seem to get sick without any regard to our work schedule. They require babysitters whether one is available or not. They demand to be "part of the action" of our lives and expect us to be part of theirs.

Put succinctly, they require sacrifices. There is simply no other way to provide them with proper care and supervision. Is it any surprise then that many adults, whose primary commitment is to themselves, are unwilling to make the sacrifices children require?

If parents will not make the sacrifices to care properly for their children, who will? It seems that the children themselves will. They will sacrifice a piece of their childhood in order that their parents might attain their personal goals.

As more and more parents of both sexes determine to pursue those personal goals above all others, "Children become something of a burden and it is deemed best that their childhood end as early as possible."[7]

Children are an inconvenience to many adults today and scientific technology has risen to the challenge once again. Many of the "inconveniences" of life in previous generations have been eliminated by modern technology. Illnesses such as polio and smallpox have been conquered. Slow and unsafe modes of travel have been replaced by high-speed trains and planes. Much of the drudgery of housekeeping has been eliminated by modern appliances.

So it remained for technology to eliminate, or at least reduce as much as possible, the inconvenience to adult careers and lifestyles caused by children. The birth control pill, introduced to widespread use in the 1960s, was the first and most successful weapon in the war against the inconvenience of children.

The pill and other related technological advances meant that for the first time sex could be separated from procreation. For the first time, couples were free to choose when, if ever, to have children. That choice, like many of life's choices, was a complicated one.

An uncooperative economy seemed to be frustrating the personal economic goals of many couples. They wanted more freedom to work and work harder in pursuit of those goals. Often they felt as if there were only one choice: children or a comfortable lifestyle.[8] The falling birth rate and declining family size between 1970 and 1985 is dramatic evidence of the choice many couples made.

During the same period, technology gave couples another choice. If the new birth control technology failed, there was a "fail-safe" mechanism: abortion.

Since the U.S. Supreme Court conferred a general legality on abortion in 1973, there have been an estimated 4000 abortions *each day*. That adds up to 1.5 million annually and nearly 20 million over the period 1973 to 1987.[9]

Twenty-five years ago, many of those 20 million aborted children would have been allowed to be born. They would have been born into a world where they were their parents' pride and joy, the objects of their parents' sacrifices, and the bearers of their parents' hopes for the future. But today they would have been born into a world where they would be seen as an economic liability, an inconvenience, an obstacle to self-fulfillment. Thus they were not allowed to be born at all.

Daddy, Can I Help?

I woke up on Saturday morning. The sun was bright, the air was fresh, and I was ready to plunge into the work of the day. My list of simple, yet necessary little handyman tasks was waiting!

A quick check of the list was encouraging. If I got right to it and worked steadily, I would be done in time for the early afternoon football game. But just then I heard the sound that strikes despair into the heart of any father wanting to get through his chores quickly. A little voice called out, "Daddy, can I help?" It was time to slow down, revise my plans, and make time to include my young son.

Children have certain minimum economic requirements for adequate health, safety, and overall care, to be sure. Certainly, they, like adults, appreciate a new toy now and then and pleasant, comfortable clothes and surroundings. Most parents know all too well the financial sacrifices they require. But when all is said and done, "What they'll remember most about their childhood when they grow older are two things: how much love was in the home and how much time you spent with them."[10]

Time is perhaps the biggest sacrifice a young child requires of the parents. This sacrifice, however, delays or defeats the steady march up a career ladder. It defers the pleasure of a good book or even a few moments with one's spouse.

But time is the one currency which we all possess in equal amount. It is the currency of life itself. Time is a treasure, and Jesus might well have said of time, as he did of material goods, where your time is, "there your heart will be also."[11]

Most married couples can reach back into the dim memories of their dating years. Remember when you could not wait to see him or her? Then, when the date ended, it was always too soon. There was never enough time to be with the one you love!

In that sense time is a real measure of our love. And that is why many children today, even those whose parents provide for them economically, have reason to grieve the loss of their parents' love and care.

Do we Americans *really* care less for children? There are some other depressing bits of evidence. Not only are we having fewer children but we are spending less time with them. Recent research shows that fathers spend about thirty-seven seconds each day, on the average, with their preschool children. By the time these children reach junior high school, fathers are spending slightly over one minute per day (7.5 per week).[12] One scholar asserts that "parents in this country spend less time with their children than in any other nation in the world, perhaps with the exception of England—the one country that surpasses the U.S. in violent crimes and juvenile delinquency."[13]

Preschool children are the hardest hit by the loss of time with parents. Young children, especially, require a lot of parental time—time listening, time reflecting with the child on his or her feelings and experiences, time focusing on the child and his or her growing world. There may possibly be such a thing as a good "One-Minute Manager," but it is impossible to be an adequate "One-Minute Parent" to a child of any age! Parenting requires the sacrifice of time.

How much time *do* young children require? There is some validity to the old saying that it is not the quantity but the quality of time spent with our children that counts. Every married person knows that you can be near or with someone in the same room or house for a long quantity of time of dubious quality!

Time, expressed as love, is the most fundamental ingredient in developing and maintaining healthy relationships between spouses or between parents and children. As one wise family counselor put it, "Time is like oxygen. There's a minimal amount that is needed to survive. Less than that amount may cause permanent damage. And I think the same holds true for a child's time and exposure to both parents."[14]

It is not easy for parents to find this kind of quality (and quantity) time and energy to spend with their young children today. The increase in two-career families often means a substantial decrease in the total amount of time and energy that parents have left to spend with their children.

Parents are so busy today. Fathers work long hours to compete in the "dog eat dog" business world. Working mothers often have to work harder to compete in what is still, too often, a man's world in the marketplace. Couples do want to get ahead economically, not just stay even. They want to be able to do things their friends can afford. They want the self-esteem that a successful career brings. Some have clearly chosen to put personal material goals (the vacation home, the European vacation, and so on) ahead of the needs of their children for the time, attention, and nurture of their parents.

"Yes," but other parents say, "we need two full-time incomes just to make ends meet. It's just not as easy for us economically. We *have* to have two full-time incomes."

No doubt for some families that is true. A special circumstance may limit the income capacity of one spouse so that both need to work full time outside the home. And women who want to work outside the home must, of course, be fully entitled to do so. Single mothers, struggling valiantly to keep off welfare and out of poverty, would consider two incomes a real luxury!

But is it economically *necessary* to have two full-time incomes today to keep the family fed and clothed in a modest middle-class fashion? Are parents *forced* to spend less and less time with their children for economic reasons or are they choosing to do so for personal reasons?

As you might suspect, I believe that for many families today the answer is that parents are choosing to spend less time with their children to devote themselves to the pursuit of personal, often economic, goals. The myth that poor economic policies or inflation are somehow forcing more and more women into the workplace and forcing fathers to work longer and harder is just that, a myth.

While it is true that the rate of growth of family income has slowed somewhat in recent years, it is still rising. Family income has risen by one-third since 1970 and by one-tenth since 1980 (though the overall rate of growth since 1970 is only about one-half that of the 1960s). It is still on the way up.[15]

In addition to a growing income, families are smaller now than a generation ago, so more money goes to support fewer people. There have also been significant gains in the fringe benefits provided most wage earners. Surely, there should be little to complain about.

Yet fewer Americans were satisfied with their economic circumstances in 1986 than in 1956. Many young adults in their twenties and thirties complain that they are not as well off financially as their parents were. They do not feel they can afford to maintain the standard of living they remember from childhood.

If you ask the typical baby boomer (twenty-five to forty years old) whether he or she is living better than his or her parents, the answer is likely to be "My head says yes but my heart says no."[16] Even if you remind the person that today well over 40 percent of American families own two cars compared to 15 percent in 1960 and that VCRs were not even invented then, he or she is still dissatisfied.

The problem is not one of the head, logic, or even economic reality. In strictly economic terms, families *are* better off economically today than ever before, even families with only one income.[17]

The problem is one of the heart. Far from being *forced* by the economy to pursue two full-time careers in order to provide for their families, many couples choose to do so to provide for their own constantly rising economic expectations. Their frustrated expectations of an affluent lifestyle far beyond anything their parents or grandparents knew rob them of the satisfaction of enjoying what they do have, including their children. Even Christian couples who have bought the line of the "health and wealth" gospel ("God wants you rich") have suffered that loss.

Having enough is an elusive goal that stays constantly just beyond the reach of many American families today. So both parents work longer and harder than ever, juggling the increasing demands of two full-time careers. That is the choice these parents have made.

What choice do their children have? Nobody asked them if they would rather have a second car and bigger house and go to day care all day instead of staying at home with a parent and taking their afternoon nap in their own bed. Nobody asked them if they would prefer a vacation home at the beach and not having Dad around much instead of having him there to play a game most evenings and tuck them in bed at night.

Nobody gave these children a choice. Their parents expect them to be "good little soldiers" and make the sacrifices asked of them. So they do. They really have no choice.

Time spent together, parents with children, is one of the building blocks of healthy families. Talking together, working together, playing together, and worshiping together all provide children with that sense of belonging and emotional intimacy with their parents that is crucial to their emotional health. Such intimacy, however, takes time to develop.

Josh McDowell of Campus Crusade for Christ blames this lack of intimacy with one's parents for many of the emotional problems of youth and young adults today. He says the sexual revolution is really a revolution in the search of this intimacy. Most youth do not want sex, he says, but intimacy: "Young people are crying out for intimacy. Why? They're not getting it at home."[18] Developing intimacy requires a good *quantity* of time that is also good *quality* time.

Parents are deliberately choosing to spend less and less time nurturing their young children. Many adults today clearly care less for children. As a result, this care-less society is asking more and more children to care for themselves.

Only a generation or two ago, proper care of elementary and even young adolescent children was understood to mean careful supervision. It meant that parents knew where their children were, what they were doing, and supervised those activities, either in person or through another responsible adult.

Today, however, the high divorce rate and the rise of two-career families has substantially diverted much adult attention away from the careful supervision of children and onto other matters. The result is a new parental casualness toward the careful supervision of children. It is likely that, as a result, parents today provide less supervision for their school-age children than was the case even a decade ago.[19]

"I just can't stay home and guard them every minute. I have my own life to lead" was the plea of one divorced, single mother who found her thirteen and nine year olds watching pornographic movies on late-night cable television.[20] This decline in adult supervision may well be, as Marie Winn asserts, connected to early involvement by children in drugs and sexual experimentation.

The combination of unsupervised children and the highly charged sexual atmosphere we live in today has proven dangerous to many young children. Without the caring, careful supervision of adults, the temptations and corresponding opportunities to yield to them are often too great for children to withstand.

The problem is that many adults, under their own pressures, with their own lives to lead, do not seem to care. So the children have to care for themselves. That is especially true for many latch-key children today.

Self-Care or No Care

Every weekday around 3:15 P.M., my youngest son arrives home from elementary school. He bursts in the door and immediately begins to give his mother a minute-by-minute description of his day at school. He is always proud of the work papers he brings home to show her and even tells on himself if he had to sit in the "quiet chair" in class. But his excited voice conveys his pride in recounting the events of the day.

My wife has learned that nothing less than her full attention will do during these few after school moments. But they are only a relative few. Then it's a quick snack and another rush out the door to play with his friends until dinner. Only a bruised knee or bicycle accident brings him back to her, and then only for a quick fix up.

Just down the street from us, and in countless other homes around the country, the scene is strikingly different. Millions of children arrive home from school every day to be greeted only by silence. Some open the door cautiously, even fearfully. They do not rush in to be greeted by a parent, but walk in slowly, anxiously checking for strange noises or intruders.

There is no one to talk to, and the silence is frightening. They turn on the television or stereo because noise is comforting. Then they begin their wait. They are alone, taking care of themselves for an hour or two, sometimes more, until a parent gets home.

Latch-key children are not an entirely new phenomenon. Nearly half a century ago, the American Association of School Administrators expressed their concern for "door-key" children.[21] At that time, in 1943, many mothers worked during the day in defense plants and many fathers were in the service.

But after the war these door-key children became once again an oddity, recognized as a temporary, forced concession to national survival. As were the majority of children in day care, door-key children were overwhelmingly children of poor, single mothers who had to work. Since they were not a concern of most working- or middle-class families, these door-key children and the problems they faced returned to anonymity.

But the situation has changed drastically in the past decade. The number of latch-key children is growing, and many are children of solidly, middle-class, two-career families. For these families, "self-care" is definitely a choice, not a necessity.

There may be as many as 5 million children ages five to thirteen years old who come home after school to an empty house and are responsible for self-care for periods of one to three hours daily. For them it is small comfort that another 21 million (75 percent of all children five to thirteen years) are cared for by a parent after school.[22] As more and more mothers enter the work force and advance in their careers, the number of latch-key children could mushroom to 35 million by 1995.[23]

These millions of latch-key children are also victims of the care-less society. While both parents pursue full-time careers at full throttle, neither is willing to make the necessary sacrifice to provide proper care and supervision for the children after work. Unsupervised and unattended, these children are clearly in danger and at risk.

Latch-key children are not entirely alone, of course. Often their companion is fear. They hear other children talking about neighborhood break-ins and burglaries. They flinch at strange noises. They tell researchers they are afraid of being alone in stormy weather, but often they are afraid to tell their parents of their fears.

Loneliness is another frequent companion of young latch-key children. As soon as my son finishes an instant replay of the day, he is out the door to play with his friends. For most latch-key children, there is no parent there to greet them and hear about their day. Playing outside may not be permitted. They have to stay inside, alone, behind locked doors.

Whether they stay inside alone or play outside unsupervised, their constant companion is danger. The National Safety Council reports that of the 6000 children a year who die in accidents or fires at home, few have an adult present. Just when they needed a parent the most, in times of danger, none was there.

A generation ago, an adult almost always cared for children after school. It was likely Mom or Grandmother. When I was a young child, my grandmother took care of me until my mother arrived home from her job as an elementary school teacher. Today, with mothers working and the extended family a relative rarity, a growing number of parents have shifted the responsibility for after school care from competent adults to children themselves. Along the way a dangerous necessity—self-care for young children—has been made into an acceptable, commonplace practice.

Under the heading "Stories for Free Children," *Ms.* ran an article that typifies this change. The article "On My Own: Self Care for Kids at Home," gave guidelines for latch-key children to follow. The author advised them not to accept rides after school with anyone other than parents, to go straight home, to keep their key safe, and how to tell if their house is safe to enter. They were also instructed how to call the police and how to handle medical emergencies.[24]

This and a flood of similar books and articles are built on assumptions that are dubious at best and dangerous at worst. Is a nine-year-old child left home alone and unsupervised behind locked doors for two hours every day really a "free" child? More likely he or she is "free" of a precious naiveté that permits him or her to relax and play knowing that a responsible adult is nearby.

Is such a child in self-care cared for properly? Until recently, the responsibility of caring for a six- or eight-year-old child was generally felt most appropriately an adult responsibility. It was a burden too heavy for a child to carry alone.

But the increasing reliance on self-care indicates a growing feeling among adults that "it is acceptable, even desirable, for children to be regularly unsupervised after school if they have learned some basic skills."[25] They may even develop great independence and responsibility, some parents feel.

But what is the purchase price of this independence? Surveys and studies tend to confirm that latch-key children do take more responsibility for their own care, especially cooking and cleaning responsibilities. But they are also cited by their teachers as "the number one cause of problems" in the public schools.[26]

They do become more self-reliant at an earlier age, it is true. But they take on other, less desirable adult attributes, also. An Undersecretary for Health of the U.S. Department of Health and Human Services feels it is likely that the current epidemic of teenage pregnancy is compounded by the latch-key phenomenon.[27] A generation ago, teens may have received their sexual initiation at night in the backseat of a car. Today it is more likely to be in the afternoon on the living room couch.

Yale psychologist Edward Zigler, who has studied child development for thirty years, says there is a definite connection between leaving children unsupervised after school and such social problems as teen pregnancy, juvenile delinquency, and drug abuse. He observes that we adults "are really precipitating these problems if we do not provide adult supervision for children and allow them to socialize themselves and each other. Children should be in the care of adults. They do not have the ability, the cognitive wherewithal or experience to socialize themselves."[28]

Children *should* be in the care of adults. While children "learn responsibility" in self-care, adults *shirk* their responsibility to provide them proper care and supervision. For the millions of elementary age latch-key children, self-care is no care. It implies proper care and supervision when there is none. It is often, tragically, an attempt to legitimize neglect.

Providing proper care and supervision for children requires from adults a substantial sacrifice: their time. Adults who seem to care less for children, to care less about having them or spending time parenting them are less willing to make that sacrifice for their children.

In a sad and sorry switch, millions of children are sacrificing for their parents. Giving up adult care and taking on the burden of self-care, they become, as one educator put it, "the fallout of a society that emphasizes material success and personal fulfillment" more that the welfare of its children.[29]

These children sacrifice the innocence of childhood and take on the stress of accepting premature (adult) responsibilities for their own care and supervision. Such stress, as we have seen, puts them at risk for developing later social and emotional problems.

The physical risks of this lack of supervision are real. But so are the social risks. One educator estimates that 90 percent of children in detention centers are from the ranks of the frequently unsupervised.[30]

Christian Parents Face the Squeeze

This radical shift in adult care for children presents a special challenge to Christian parents. They, no less than other parents, often feel squeezed between the demands of maintaining two full-time careers, a comfortable life style, and the sacrifices demanded in the name of adequate care and supervision for their children.

Christian parents, no less than others, must live and make their way in a society that clearly cares less for children than any time in the last century and a half. What peculiar perspectives do they bring, as Christians, to meet these challenges?

Most basically, the Christian faith radically opposes the devaluation of children. All who, like children, are powerless and vulnerable are of special concern to Almighty God. He will be their champion when even their parents desert them.

Far from being an obstacle to personal fulfillment, an economic liability, or even an inconvenience, a child is a sign of God's blessing. He or she is a precious gift from a loving Heavenly Father. He is the one who loves each child intimately and deeply, formed each one, and knew each one while it was still in its mother's womb. [31]

Children are a special tool of God in the lives of their parents. They teach us so much about ourselves and about God, the Father. Couples who choose to be childless lose more than offspring. Poet Luci Shaw describes it this way:

> I wonder, sometimes, about young people today who choose to be childless. In their concern for career, comfort, convenience, for personal self development, may they be depriving themselves of one of God's most effective teaching tools? Had I lived without the singing joy as well as the devastating pain of being a parent, my understanding and appreciation of God the Father would have been drastically limited. [32]

What a gift children give us, to know more deeply and to understand the heart of God, the Father! He who cares for us cares also for our children. As a steward before God for the lives of those children, how can we do less for them than whatever their care requires? Has He done any less for us?

Does that mean we must make sacrifices? Yes, of course. But that is no surprise or shock. The Christian faith is built on sacrifice. God the Father sacrificed His only child—His Son Jesus—for the salvation of each of us and all of us.

Sacrificing for *our* children, then, does not sound as strange as it might to ears less familiar with the story of Jesus. Careers are important, but not ultimately. Fulfillment is important, but is not found in self alone. Time is precious, but there is always enough for our children, just as God is always there for us.

Because Christian parents understand these things (or is it *if* Christian parents understand these things?) they can make the significant and constant sacrifices their young children require. But from the perspective of faith, the sacrifices, like children, are small indeed.

The commitment to make the necessary sacrifices to care for children has been seriously eroded in America today. Instead of sacrificing for our children, we are asking them to sacrifice for us. They pay a heavy price for our personal fulfillment and affluence.

Sadly, our children "seem to accept the argument of quality time as a substitute for enough time. They act worldly wise and self reliant, as they withdraw into themselves. They make us believe that they need us only as much as we are willing to be present for them. They hurt quietly."[33]

Faced with this hurt, many adults seemingly could care less. Now we turn to examine what influences have produced this unfeeling, uncaring attitude toward children.

SEVEN:

Finding Fulfillment: The Losses to Children

Hansel and Gretel could not have suspected anything. The gingerbread house looked inviting; the old lady seemed sweet. But even in fairy tales things are not always the way they seem. Danger awaited the children.

Things are not always as they seem in the real world. Children seem as important as ever. Many adults want their own children desperately. Surrogate mothers and test-tube babies testify eloquently to that. But inside this sweet, appealing "gingerbread house" of love for children, lurk a number of trends and attitudes that are dangerous to children, creating an antichild atmosphere.

This antichild atmosphere, just below the surface of American society, threatens to rob children of some of the things they need most from adults. Children are devalued, suffer a loss of caring, and lack the importance to motivate parents to sacrifice for their needs.

Robert Ringer's 1971 bestseller, *Looking Out for Number One*, pointed to the basic element in this antichild atmosphere: self-centeredness as a legitimate lifestyle. Ringer's book spells out his concept of the meaning of life clearly and directly: to live in such a way as to ensure that you are as happy as possible. Look out for yourself and your own interests first. Everything (and everyone) else is only a means to that end.[1]

Ringer's book both reflected and helped to promote the acceptance in our society of what could be called a (secular) religion of self. Some call it individualism. Individualism's god is myself (I'm number 1!) and its gospel is selfishness without guilt.[2] Its perverted "holy trinity" is me, myself, and I.

"Do your own thing" became the slogan of the 1970s because doing one's thing was seen as the key to happiness and fulfillment. But doing one's thing requires liberation from all limits in order to be free to choose what that thing really is! From that perspective, true fulfillment in life is freedom to look out for number 1, selfishly and without guilt!

This attitude has permeated all relationships, including the family. In 1972 George and Nena O'Neill hailed the advent of the open marriage.[3] Open marriage freed couples from the bondage of unfulfilling commitments to each other. Of course, upholding the stable marriages required to give children the emotional security they need was not a priority.

Immediate self-fulfillment has indeed become the measure of a successful marriage for many couples today. One woman interviewed by sociologist Robert Bellah explained her understanding of a marriage relationship this way: "If other people don't meet your needs, you have to be willing to walk out, since in the end, that may well be the only way to protect your interests."[4]

Bellah's research shows how depressingly common this attitude is.

The kind of marriage that results when two such self-centered individuals base their relationship on individual self-fulfillment can only be a commitment of convenience. It is often a case of "love by contract," with perhaps a little romance thrown in.

The ease and frequency of divorce today attest to the degree to which many marriages are little more than "a freely contracted arrangement between consenting adults."[5] As long as you meet my needs, the "contract is in force." If I am not being fulfilled, however, I will probably walk out, since "that may well be the only way to protect my interests" (the only interests that really matter to me).

What this means to the children of these marriages is obvious. Marriage is demeaned and devalued by these attitudes. As a result, children, who depend on the quality and stability of a marriage for their emotional and spiritual health, are also devalued. Their needs and welfare take second place to those of the marriage partners.

What part did the children play in establishing this marriage contract? None, of course. Their parents set the terms of the marriage: their own self-fulfillment, the measure of all things. That is the end to which even the children must contribute. Somewhere in all of this, the unique value and needs of the children themselves got lost![6]

In fact, children can undermine this kind of marriage. One feminist put it bluntly: "No amount of sweetness and light, innocence or charm, can outweigh the fact that they are a pain . . . and cost a lot of money."[7] Children require so much from their parents—time, money, care, and supervision. All this militates *against* the realization of their parents' personal careers or lifestyle goals and self-fulfillment.

This kind of marriage, held together by mutual self-love, is neither safe nor congenial to raising children. That mutual self-love would certainly be a strange kind of love to the writer of 1 Corinthians 13. All relationships are urged to strive toward the love described there. It is love that is patient, kind, able to endure hardships, and able to wait for its rewards. Most striking of all, it is not self-seeking; rather it seeks the good of others.

This kind of love, the writer says, provides a lasting, stable base on which to build a truly fulfilling relationship. That love always perseveres, endures, and never fails, whatever the situation. What a bold contrast to the weak self-love on which so many marriages are built today![8]

Motivated by this self-giving love, marriage partners are willing to sacrifice self-interest when it is necessary for the good of the marriage or the children. These are not unhealthy "child-centered" marriages where parents sacrifice their own relationship in favor of their children. These are healthy "other-centered" relationships of real, giving love. By contrast partners motivated by self-love have no basis for understanding how love can imply sacrifice. If you love someone, it is no sacrifice to please that person, and if sacrifice to one's self is required, it cannot be love![9]

It is easy to see why children suffer from this pervasive search for self-fulfillment, this fascination with selfishness without guilt. Shallow, inevitably unfulfilling, unstable marriages result. And children, who were never a central priority of the marriage anyway, suffer as a consequence.

Such marriage contracts are surely harmful to children. Contracts are easily broken; ask any lawyer. They are better replaced with marriage "covenants." Covenants are permanent commitments of each partner to the other and are not dependent on self-fulfillment or "your meeting my needs," but on self-giving love.

Children need the blessing of growing up in families where marriages are based on such covenants. They need the security of growing up in families where love is understood as a "permanent commitment with obligations that transcend the immediate feelings or wishes" of the members.[10]

Marriages built on this kind of love—a biblical love that reflects God's own love for His people—are marriages that last. They are marriages where love perseveres, "settles in for the long haul," is not self-seeking and is willing to wait for its reward and to sacrifice for the good of others.

This marriage can provide for children what they need and deserve. Sadly, individualism has robbed children of the security of strong marriages and relegated them to a lesser place in the family. Individualism has been a major factor contributing to parents' growing unwillingness to nurture and care personally for their young children.

Individualism and Male Careerism

When mothers began streaming out of the home and into the workplace, often putting their infants into day care for fifty hours or more each week, where were these children's fathers? The fathers were right where they and other fathers before them had always been—in the workplace earning their family's living.

Of course, for many men, their jobs represent more than just an income. Ask a man who he is and he will likely reply, "I'm a dentist," "I'm a salesclerk," or "I'm a steelworker." His first response will be to define himself by his job, not by his relationships. It is a rare man who answers that question by saying, "I'm a husband and father!"

This is one of the facts of life tied up with the traditional sex roles and cultural assumptions of our society. A man *is* what he does; his worth is measured by his success at it. Success, in turn, is measured by such things as salary, responsibilities, recognition, awards, and other tangible and intangible factors.

So how does a man who wants to be self-fulfilled and look out for number 1 pursue that goal? He does it through success at his job. His devotion to careerism may mean virtual neglect of his wife and children. It may require moving every three years to keep advancing in the company (while his family has no roots in a community). No matter; this is the price many men and their families pay so that Dad can be successful. After all, is not that what fathers are supposed to be?

The stories are legion of men, even Christian leaders, who gave themselves so totally to their jobs that their marriages crumbled and their children became emotionally crippled. For other families, heroic women gave themselves unselfishly to try to be both Mom and Dad for their children. Somehow, wonderfully, the children turned out all right!

Don't get me wrong. Those were *not* the good old days. They certainly were not good for anyone, for father, mother, or children. But they *are* old in the sense that, increasingly, they do not happen today. Dad may still be caught up in careerism, seeking self-fulfillment in his work. But Mom will not likely be at home to pick up the pieces anymore. Individualism has also spoken to her through the voice of feminism. Now she is out seeking *her* identity in the workplace right alongside Dad.

Feminism, Mothers, and Fulfillment

She is a working woman. Up before dawn most days, she cooks breakfast for her family before reviewing her schedule for the day. She is competent and capable at what she does. During the day she demonstrates her managerial and executive skills in a number of ways.

Her day is full of such things as managing finances, buying and selling, and working on behalf of the poor and needy. Often, she is at work long into the evening. And on top of everything else, she makes her own clothes!

She manages to take good care of her family and her household. It is no surprise that this woman is highly respected in the community as both a wise and accomplished woman. One may be surprised, however, to learn that she is a stay-at-home mother and homemaker.

This woman is described in the Bible in Proverbs 31. It is a fresh reminder that working women, especially working mothers (is there any other kind?), are nothing new at all. Across the centuries women have worked in and around the home. In doing so, they were essential and integral to their family's economic well-being, whether in ancient Israel, medieval Europe, or frontier America.

One of my wife's friends gave her an inscribed apron that summed it up nicely: "All mothers are working mothers." With one major exception—single mothers whose work is a daily battle with poverty—there is a significant difference between working women of the past and those of today, however.

Today more and more women, including mothers of infants and young children, are choosing to work *outside* the home. Nearly one-half of all women with children under eighteen work outside the home, double the percentage of thirty years ago. Unlike their sisters of earlier generations, these women have been able to choose whether to pursue a career and, if so, to pursue it outside the home.

This freedom to choose to pursue a career outside the home is one of the positive results of the feminist movement. Feminism grew up in the fertile soil of the individualism of the 1960s and 70s. It shares common roots with the civil rights movement and other rights movements of the time. Feminism challenged women to seek *their* rights, especially their right to self-fulfillment, to being all that they could be.

Betty Friedan sounded the clarion call of feminism in *The Feminine Mystique* published in the early 1960s. Women, she charged, were trapped by social expectations that they be passive, dependent, noncompetitive, and defined primarily by their relationships to men. A woman's role in life was "restricted to timeless, changeless love and service of husband and children," Friedan said.[11]

How could these women be fulfilled, asked Friedan, if they were trapped into "living through their husbands and children instead of finding their individual identity" in the world?[12] The time had come for women to seek their own identity and their own fulfillment by accepting the challenges and responsibilities of full and equal participation in the mainstream of American political, economic, and social life.[13]

Whatever one's feelings about feminism, there can be no doubt of its influence, even on many women who reject much of its antimale, antifamily language. Many middle-class, college-educated women found a reason and a justification to break out of their "domestic prison" and get out "where the action is," the workplace.

"What to others must seem a lovely home, to me is both a prison and an endless treadmill," wrote one depressed full-time mother.[14] Full-time mothers, especially those with more than one small child at home, are as much at risk of burnout as any pastor or high pressured businessman.

My wife was an elementary teacher in the Pittsburgh, Pennsylvania, city school system when I met her. She had been a successful teacher for five years before we were married in 1971. She decided that after our wedding she would not go back to work. She was going to stay home and devote herself exclusively to keeping house for her new husband. It sounded good to me!

A couple months passed before we both made an important discovery. We had no children, and there are only so many times each week you need to clean a one-bedroom apartment! My wife knew she needed to find some other meaningful activity. So she returned to doing one of the things she does best—teaching young children—until our first son was born.

Where Is That Proverbs Woman Now?

It is more difficult to be a Proverbs 31 woman today, to find a significant outlet for entrepreneurial and managerial skills within the home and experience adult companionship and stimulation. Modern appliances have drastically reduced much of the time and energy (as well as the drudgery) of housekeeping.

In contrast to preindustrial days, our economy functions largely outside and independent of the home. Cottage industries from the home are anachronisms; real work is done in the public workplace. It is hard to convince a college-educated young woman that "running the washing machine is as creative, scientific and challenging as solving the genetic code."[15]

Mothers who, against these odds, bravely choose to stay at home with their young children still face the awful isolation of much of American family life. The decline of the extended family means grandmother and even an aunt or two are not around for companionship during the long day. This aloneness is compounded by the deliberate isolation of many suburban homes and the anonymity of much of city life.

Thus when feminists called women to pursue their own brand of male individualism and find their identity and fulfillment by joining men at work, conditions had created an audience of willing listeners. Feminism called women to seek their salvation in the same way men had always done: at work outside the home. That is where the real business of life is carried out, feminists argued, and that is where its true rewards (the only ones that count) are earned.

Why Work?

Chances are that if you could measure a man's self-esteem, the strength of it would be based on his perception of his job success. The visible signs of that success are salary, awards, promotions, and so on. Feminists assert that a woman's worth is based to no less a degree on her productivity in the public work world. This assumption is widely accepted among women today.

One woman spoke of the tangible self-esteem she felt from her career in the marketplace. At home no one ever told her "that's a great dry diaper" or "those dishes are really clean." On the other hand, her full-time job offers her the satisfaction of tangible rewards—greater responsibility, promotions, and salary increases.[16]

As intentionally as that woman chose to seek fulfillment in the work world, however, other women have chosen to stay at home and care for their young children as *their* full-time career. Despite the routine, despite the apparent lack of recognition, most are proud and happy to do so.

Still, some of these women do feel lonely. They may be the only woman at home on the entire block for most of every workday. Other women feel another, even more acute kind of loneliness.

One full-time mother who chose to stay home to care for her young children, largely because of her Christian commitment, felt cut off from the understanding and support of much of the Christian community. Churches spend thousands of dollars on day-care centers but nothing on ministries to mothers who stay at home with their children. Wouldn't it be great, she mused, if those day-care centers offered one free day of child care each week to women who are full-time mothers?[17]

This mother shares the frustration that has driven many of her friends out of the home into the marketplace. These women all "feel sharply the lack of respect shown by a materialistic society to an occupation that pays no salary, and in which there are no higher positions for which to compete."[18] Sadly, women who devote themselves to a career of full-time care and nurture of their children share the fate of comedian Rodney Dangerfield. They "get no respect, no respect at all."

That desire for respect, self-esteem, and a sense of fulfillment has, as much as anything, propelled many mothers into the full-time work world. Many single mothers have no choice in the matter, of course, and some women, faced with the high divorce rate, see a career as economic prudence.

But for many other women, a career outside the home is not primarily a matter of economic necessity, of keeping the family fed and clothed. It is more a matter of knocking down the doors of the "domestic prison," and going in search of self-fulfillment and a comfortable lifestyle.

One woman, a secretary, said she worked so that she and her husband could "get ahead, not just stay even" financially. Her husband put it this way: "Kathy works not to pay the mortgage on the house but to put furniture in it."

A preschool teacher gave a similar reason for her career. She works outside the home to buy the extras she and her husband enjoy: going out, buying gifts, traveling and sending their daughter to dance, drama, and craft classes.

"No one cares how well I vacuum the floor," said one woman. "And I really enjoy working. It's challenging and I feel as though I have a lot of responsibility."[19]

Women, like men, find challenge, fulfillment, and tangible rewards in the work world. One woman, an executive with a marketing agency, described her feelings about her job this way: ". . . I like working. It's not an economic necessity. But I don't think I would be happy staying at home. I need to feel like I'm doing something on my own."[20]

Whatever its drawbacks (and there definitely *are* some), feminism has provided a valuable service to women. It has given voice to many of their frustrations and helped open up the public work world as an alternative and additional source of fulfillment, status, and independence. Are not women *entitled* equally with men to choose such a public career and compete equally with them in the marketplace? The answer must be an enthusiastic "yes!"

Feminism and Children

The impact of feminism has been much less positive on another party, however. In fact, an examination of the impact of feminism on young children changes the whole focus of the discussion. "The question of the care and upbringing of children is the crux of the whole sex role debate, which should really be called the child debate, since it is the children who in the last resort are most concerned."[21]

Those who care for children *should* be concerned with some feminist goals and values. They reflect a definite antichild bias. One feminist writer, for example, praised the virtues of being a woman who is "child-free" (to state it positively) as opposed to being "child-less." She called having one's own biological children today "irresponsible."

Rather, she said, those who are child-free should help care for existing children. In this way the line between the biological and nonbiological mother begins to disappear. The nuclear family is oppressive and children are a burden. This is one way to lighten that burden.[22]

Motherhood, to some feminists, is a totally negative situation. Child rearing is an obstacle to full equality with men. Only when it is possible to break this "tyranny of the biological family" and shorten to the minimum the period of the dependence of young children on their parents, will women begin to be free; some feminists assert.[23]

It is hard to see how an aggressive proabortion stance can be interpreted as anything but antichild. Abortion as an unfettered, individual choice for all women is, of course, a firm plank in the platform of the National Organization for Women (NOW), the leading feminist group.

NOW also aggressively supports equal opportunity for women to find fulfillment through employment and the availability of good quality, low-cost day care for children. These are clearly less dubious goals than unrestricted abortion and breaking "the tyranny of the biological family" over women, for example.

But for infants and preschool children, the issue of feminism is not whether their mothers are free to work full time outside the home or whether they find self-fulfillment and self-esteem in their careers. Perhaps mothers working full time outside the home *are* happier and more fulfilled. But at what price?

For their young children, the price is the loss of care, nurturing, and interaction with their mothers (which loss has, in most cases, not been made up by fathers). Another loss is that they have had to "endure an earlier and even longer separation from intimate family contacts" while they spend their days in the care of strangers.[24]

Infants and toddlers especially require a lot of parental time, energy, and sacrifice. David Elkind cites the need for parental "decentering" away from their own immediate needs and desires to those of their children as much as possible.[25] This "decentering" is what enables a parent to give an abundance of time and nurturing to a young, demanding child.

Every year, however, more and more women take their places in the public marketplace alongside men. Both sexes now draw much of their essential identity and satisfaction from the same source, work. As this continues, and if conditions within families remain unchanged, there is likely to be a continued decline in the quantity and quality of care given by parents to their young children.

In the face of such unrestrained careerism (career first) and individualism (me first) by both men and women, children will be viewed more and more as an obstacle to personal fulfillment. Childhood dependency will seem even more an outmoded, unaffordable luxury.[26]

Are Working Moms Really So Bad?

The movement of more and more mothers of young children into the public workplace in the last quarter century has been a real revolution. As with any revolution, it has been accompanied by sharp, even angry debate. Is it really so bad for children?

Some champions of working mothers (*remember:* all mothers are working mothers!) point to real benefits to the children when their moms work full time outside the home. Their children are often more independent earlier in life and they may also get better grades. Although such mothers might have felt guilty in the past, now "it turns out that perhaps they should feel guilty if they stay home," some experts say.[27]

Those who oppose mothers of young children working full time outside the home are not convinced. They are likely to agree with the Harvard professor who feels that "young children of mothers working full time are at a significant disadvantage emotionally and intellectually" compared to children of full-time mothers.[28]

So who is right? Though it is not easy to say, both sides must be listened to carefully. The future of a couple of generations of children is at stake. Some early studies, beginning to be completed, offer some preliminary answers.

One of the most widely quoted recent studies of children of working mothers was conducted by researchers at the University of Akron (Ohio). Their results were hailed as among the first to show that having a working mother actually produces benefits to young children.[29]

These researchers studied 573 first, third, and fifth graders in 38 states. Nearly two-thirds had mothers who worked outside the home; the rest did not. The results indicated that children with working mothers have higher I.Q.s, get better grades, and receive higher evaluations from their teachers than children whose mothers are at home full time. They also score better for independence and self-reliance.

The one area where the children of working mothers did not show a clear advantage, the researchers said, was in regard to their closeness or emotional bonding with their mothers. This is the same problem Dr. Belsky and other researchers discovered in regard to children whose mothers returned to full-time work and put them in day care under the age of one.

These children reported that they were more likely to tell a friend or a babysitter, rather than their mothers, about their day in school or a fight with a friend. Children of mothers who are at home full time said they would tell their mothers first.

The authors of the report had an interesting approach to this potentially discouraging (to them) finding. Don't panic, mothers, they said, in effect. These children probably mentioned the name of the person physically most available to them; their answers probably didn't reflect any emotional closeness.[30]

Of course, such an explanation is possible but it seems quite unlikely. Young children do not make those kinds of distinctions. Children develop emotional ties with the people they see, hug, smell, and talk to, people who are there when needed or just wanted. They naturally come to love the one they spend the most time with day after day, whether it is a parent or a sitter.

James Dobson strongly criticized this study in his *Focus on the Family* newsletter. He pointed to what he called its "obvious bias" against the traditional family and the flawed procedure followed by the researchers.[31]

Dr. Dobson pointed out that the nonworking mother category in the study did not simply include women who, for personal or philosophical reasons, chose to stay home and care for their children. The category also included mothers who stayed home because they "had no employable skills, those who were too ill to work; those who did not speak English; those who were emotionally unstable; those who were alcoholics and drug abusers; those with low intelligence; and those who began conceiving out of wedlock at 15 years of age and are now struggling to raise six or eight children at home on welfare."[32] Children from these homes are already at a disadvantage. Including a small percentage of them in the study can significantly affect its outcome, especially with regard to I.Q., academic achievement, and behavior adjustment.

In fact, those were exactly the factors on which the researchers based their assertion that having a working mom is a benefit to young children. In reply Dr. Dobson quotes Burton White, director of the Harvard University PreSchool Project, a ten-year study of preschool children. Dr. White says his study affirms that there is simply no substitute for a mother's care when her children are small. He feels a full-time mother can be much more beneficial to a preschool child than a full-time nursery school or preschool experience.[33]

Neither Dobson nor White addresses the question of whether it is a *mother's* care that is so critical or *parental* care (including that of the father) that is at issue. They assume that such care will (and they seem to believe it should) be given by the mother, as in the traditional family model.

Nonetheless, when Mom goes to work full time something has to give. These young children, Dr. Dobson feels, "are at a significant disadvantage emotionally and intellectually" compared to children who have the benefits of the full-time care of their mothers.[34]

Dr. Dobson and others raise serious questions that ought to be of concern to all parents and people who care about young children. More (unbiased) study is certainly needed. We must proceed cautiously in the face of the wholesale withdrawal of parental care and nurture that has resulted from the flood of young mothers into the work world.

But is this flood an unmitigated disaster for young children? Probably not. Alongside all the problems raised, working mothers may offer *some* benefits to their children.

Perhaps young girls, for example, do benefit somewhat from seeing their mothers acting confidently and competently in the work world. This experience may well broaden a young girl's understanding of what she might be able to do someday. In some way it may enhance her own self-confidence and self-esteem, as proponents of working women suggest. That is certainly no disadvantage.

This argument about the "positive model" of a working mother has a qualified and limited (if real) validity. However, based on this dubious assumption, full-time mothers do not or cannot act competently in an important life venture (child development) every day. Further, this argument assumes that what both feminism and the larger culture tell women is true: There is no basis for self-confidence, self-esteem, or self-fulfillment to be found by investing oneself in the life of a young child.

There are many women who, because of temperament or some other reason, do not seem cut out to be full-time mothers. They feel a need for a different sort of challenge and situation than being a full-time mother offers. A job outside the home, even a part-time one, will probably make them happier. As a result, perhaps they may be able to give better, if less, care and nurture to their young children.

But whether or not a woman works ouside the home today is probably not the critical factor in determining the effect on her young children. More likely, there are at least three critical factors: the age of the child when the mother returns to work, the time demands of the job, and the involvement of the father.

We have already seen how child development experts emphasize the importance of early nurture of a young child. The first year is especially critical and some experts say the first three years. These are the formative years of a young child's physical, emotional, and spiritual life. Mothers have traditionally provided children a wealth of stimulating, nurturing experiences during early childhood.

Today, nearly half of all working mothers return to work before their child's first birthday. This rich period of early nurture is being radically and continually shortened. For many children, it has been eliminated altogether. The director of a day-care center near where I work showed me a number of infants who came when the center opened at 7:00 A.M. each day and left when it closed at 6:00 P.M.

These babies were probably awakened shortly after 6:00 A.M., fed, dressed, and taken off to day care. In the evening they got home in time for a quick meal, a bath, and bed. One suspects they had little time with their parents.

It is unrealistic to expect their mothers to be able to give them much time, even limited quality time. To make a case that these young children benefit somehow from their mothers' careers would be difficult "when their mothers work 40–50 hours per week in outside careers and then come home exhausted to cook the meals, wash the clothes, bathe the baby, help with the homework and try to meet the emotional needs of every member of the family."[35] During those early years of life, children benefit from full-time nurture. Today, however, they often do not receive it for even a few months.

Women who have and enjoy a part-time job, one that can be done largely at home or has flexible hours, often have the best of both worlds. My wife's brother is a forensic chemist working in a major metropolitan crime lab and his wife is an attorney. They have two young children. When her children were in their preschool years, she intentionally limited her legal practice to a field that allowed her to limit and manage her time commitment. Much of her work was done at home on a computer and scheduled for "off-peak" child-care hours.

In fact, studies have shown that many women with part-time or flexible jobs are often the happiest of all working mothers. They have the satisfaction (and income) of a career and still enjoy a significant amount of time with their young children, time perhaps enriched by the rewards of their jobs.[36]

For some women, especially single mothers, a part-time job is not a real option, however. They need a full-time income and many jobs are not flexible.

A recent survey of mothers who work full time showed that 70 percent would prefer a part-time job or sharing a job even though they would lose income as a result.[37] Feminists promoting the interests of working women and employers looking for qualified, satisfied employees could unite to promote more part-time jobs, shared jobs, and jobs with flexible schedules. This would accommodate the many mothers of young children who choose to or must work outside the home, but want to spend more time with their young children.

This solution will not appeal to every woman. A part-time career as a doctor or lawyer, a shared job as an executive, or a career delayed for four years or more while the children are young may seem too much of a sacrifice to some women (as it probably does to most men). We are again up against the hard choice: Will it be my children first or my career?

It needs to be repeated loud and clear. In a free and pluralistic society such as ours, the simple principle of justice and fairness to which Christians, first of all, would subscribe, requires that women have the opportunity to choose freely (unless economics leave no choice) whether or not to work outside the home. They must be free to choose the option they deem best for them and their families.

But what happens when, as we have seen, those options represent choices that appear to benefit *either* a mother *or* her children, but not both? Is it fair to blame the loss of care and nurture for young children primarily on their mothers?

After all, women have traditionally carried most of the burden of child rearing as well as child bearing. From prehistory through the Middle Ages to the mid-twentieth century, sex roles have remained largely unchanged. Women's work was predominantly in the private sphere of home and child care; men conducted the public activities of economics and politics.[38]

We have seen how that has changed radically in this second half of the twentieth century. The changes in the nature of the home and family, the isolation of the nuclear family, and the move of the economy outside the home are facts, and they are not likely to change soon. The forces that have moved women (even many mature Christian women) into the workplace are not likely to diminish.

To some advocates of the care of young children, this is dreadful news. I am less pessimistic, but it *is* alarming. There is only one way for children of two-career families to receive the abundance of nurture and care from their parents that is their due: through the determination of men once again to be fathers and not just progenitors of their children.

No other solution presents itself today. Fathers who are equally committed to the rightness of their wives' careers and meeting the needs of their young children must share with their wives a full and equal measure of the joys and responsibilities of parenthood. Fathers must face, *together with their wives*, the career versus care choices that children require.

We fathers have not been willing to do that, in most cases. When we play "Mr. Mom" for a few hours or a day, we experience fully the routine and frustrating aspects of parenthood. But is that *all* parenthood offers? Hardly any mother would say that. In those many and varied hours with her children, in all the multifaceted experiences of her young child's life, she finds those special, sparkling moments of reward. But it takes time with the child; it takes being there.

No doubt there are similar riches to be found in fatherhood. Fatherhood offers real privileges and rewards (as well as duties and sacrifices), as motherhood does. Perhaps many men must try it to like it. But first we have to try it.

Few would argue with researchers who assert that "a father's involvement definitely benefits a child's development."[39] This may be one indirect advantage (or should we say, potential advantage) of having a working mother.

Summing Up

There it is then. We have briefly examined some of the antichild bias in American society today and observed its roots in the individualism that is so much a part of our contemporary thinking. We have seen how it undermines the stable marriages children need and how it has devalued children themselves. We have noted that it often makes parents less and less willing to put their children's needs first.

We have seen the largely negative impact of feminism on children and the particular struggle in which many women are involved as they leave the home to work. For women and their children, working outside the home has been a "good news, bad news" situation: good that women have greater freedom of choice and equality, bad that they have fallen into the same trap as men;

that of careerism above all. For the children who are losing time with Mom and getting nothing in return, the news is mostly bad.

One other trend harmful to children in our society in this half century needs only a brief mention and is hardly controversial. It is the accelerated secularism and moral pluralism that characterizes America today. The result is that the vast majority of the current generation of children are growing up without having to confront biblical values.

Children who grew up before World War II did not all become committed to the Christian faith and the Lord of that faith, Jesus Christ. But they were almost always forced (by dint of growing up within what was still a culture with a Christian consensus) to recognize and confront that Lord and that faith. They had to answer for themselves Christ's question to Peter, "Who do you say I am?"[40] It was hard to escape bumping into that question somewhere.

The accelerated secularism and moral pluralism of our society today has changed all that. Today it is much harder for a young child, unless from a strong Christian home, to hear the name of Christ, unless it is used as a curse. Biblical values are banned from public places where children might innocently encounter them, whether in public schools or town squares (where Christmas creches are under fire). The public square, as Richard Neuhaus observes, is naked of those enduring values.[41] Children are much, much poorer for the loss.

Clearly, all this poses some serious challenges to Christians and all people of good will who care about children as well as to the Christian church and the larger society. However, some exciting new models of parenting and caring for young children are emerging. We turn next to these.

Part II

THE HOPE

EIGHT

Hope for Restoring Lost Parenting: New Attitudes Toward Children and Careers

Y ou find them in cities all over the country. In Miami a dual-career couple has worked it out for themselves. In Pittsburgh a couple really does go half and half in work and child care. In New York a stay at home mother is also a budding entrepreneur.

These parents, and others like them, are leading a small but important movement aimed at recovering a healthy balance between the demands of work and parenting. They have rejected the widely accepted notion that fulfillment, for both sexes, is found primarily in work and that child rearing must usually take second place.

Revolutions are often spurred on by frustrations of some sort and this one is no exception. Most Americans would not argue against the equal right of every woman to choose a career outside the home. But even the most talented women with the most supportive husbands realize there are drawbacks and special challenges.

Often, the marriages of dual-career spouses are strained. Many days, each partner has only a little time late at night to give to the other. This is hardly quality, relation-building time. After a long day of work and a busy evening of household chores, "the body is exhausted, the libido is quavering and the mind is cluttered."[1] To make matters worse, one parent may work days and the other nights. Too often, there is not enough time or energy to build or maintain a strong marriage.

Women carry an especially heavy burden in these dual-career marriages because, in most cases, they still must do the great majority of the household chores. Husbands are either unwilling or unavailable (being at work most of the time) to help significantly. A career woman's exhaustion is then compounded by bitterness, and adding extra late-night chores to a tired husband's load does not seem a good solution either.

Christine Davidson in her book *Staying Home Instead*, a chronicle of her decision to work at home while caring for her young children, describes the plight of many working mothers as having replaced "their detergent box or baby bottle with the two-ton briefcase." Sometimes the demands of pursuing a full-time career while caring for young children seem that heavy.[2]

These women and their husbands in Miami, Pittsburgh, and New York and other areas around the country have made a decision and begun to act on it. They will not accept the choice of *either* career *or* care for their children, and they question the assumption that they should put careers first.

Sequencing

It is an old strategy with a modern name, *sequencing*. Some career women are turning in their two-ton briefcases to become full-time, at home mothers, at least while their children are young.

As with many women today, these mothers completed their education and gained some work experience before taking time out to have children. Most plan to resume their careers but will likely reenter the workplace (after their children enter school) with a part-time job, at least at first.[3]

My wife began sequencing nearly fifteen years ago, taking leave from her teaching position until our oldest son was ready for preschool. Then, about three and a half years later, she resumed her teaching career for six years until our youngest son was born. She took another three-and-a-half-year leave and then began her third sequence of duty at that school. In fact, sequencing is a reborn approach to balancing career and children; it is an approach used throughout much of this century.

Why do these women take time out from promising careers to be full-time parents? They decided that raising their own children is more important than having those little extras or climbing up the corporate ladder as far and as fast as possible. They have decided to strike a new balance of careers and children that weighs in on the side of children.

How do they manage it? The author of a study of women who are sequencing says two factors are critical. One is that the couple, as a couple, places a higher value on children being cared for by their own mother than on the things money can buy. These couples are willing to tighten their budgets in order to manage the loss of income.

The other critical factor is a supportive spouse.[4] Husbands who share their wives' priorities regarding maximum parental care and nurture for their young children and accept willingly the financial sacrifices make sequencing an option where everybody wins, mothers, children, and the entire family. Obviously, sequencing is a much less viable option for single mothers!

The Proverbs 31 Woman Reborn

Other women are rediscovering the biblical model of the Proverbs 31 woman. Skillfully she blended the worlds of home and work in such a way as to use her gifts, contribute to her family's economic health, and also care for her children at home.

This has been the traditional way women have chosen to balance career and children during most of history (including biblical times). Most American women followed it right up to the end of the nineteenth century.

Until the Industrial Revolution took hold in America, most families (men, women, and children) worked side by side on the family farm. The woman helped with farm work and cared for the children. She always made a significant contribution to the family economy by producing goods, such as clothing and preserved food, that the family would otherwise have to buy.

Sometimes she ran a cottage industry that produced goods to sell outside the home, or she helped her spouse run the family business (if she did not run her own). This is the role the woman of Proverbs 31 seems to have played. She made the family clothing, bought and sold real estate, and made fine clothing to be sold outside the home.

She was a true entrepreneur and a skillful manager, all the while caring for her own children at home. Hers is the most truly traditional woman's role, not the bored, stay at home mother who finds no significant thing to fill the hours of the day. The role of the Proverbs 31 woman was a "congenial blending of tasks" that included the challenge of raising children as an integral part of that role.[5]

When the Industrial Revolution took the focus of the economy out of the home and into the factory, this healthy integration of career and children, exemplified by the Proverbs 31 woman, began to disappear. Economic change made it difficult to maintain, and soon the pseudotraditional role division of woman as homemaker only and man as breadwinner only developed.

This is a relatively recent, culturally based division that is neither biblically normative (it was unknown in biblical times) nor particularly healthy. The tensions and frustrations it has caused for women have been clearly presented time and again.

But it poses serious problems for men and for children, also. Some years ago Ann Landers ran a letter from a woman whose husband (she used the pseudonym Thomas) had been debilitated by a stroke. The poor woman was understandably burdened by the weight of caring for him day after day with no relief.

She shared her plight with his three daughters by a previous marriage. Perhaps they could help out or at least provide occasional relief. She told Ann Landers of the daughters' responses. One daughter refused, one said she would take him to lunch if she happened to be in the neighborhood, and the other took him to her home to visit a few times, all the while complaining how greatly inconvenienced she was by it all.

Were the daughters to blame for such careless, selfish behavior? Perhaps so, but I cannot help agreeing with the writer who said a prior and equally pressing question was "What kind of father had this guy been, anyway, to have produced children so utterly indifferent to his welfare?"[6]

This strict woman/homemaker, man/breadwinner role division deprives men of the freedom to participate fully in the nurturing of their children, in the special joy and privilege of shaping the life and soul of another human being, their child. It is a role division from which men need liberation too.

Poor Thomas, neglected by his three daughters, may have been a victim of that role division.

> More than likely, he was simply a father like so many others in this society, one who tried, in his fashion, to make time for the kids—who helped out with birthday parties and made it to the occasional school play—but one for whom—as children themselves always learn—grown-up affairs simply mattered more than they did: the sort of father who lacks the time, the patience and finally the intensity of interest to know his children as they need to be known.[7]

Conversely, children have lost the special privilege of having a father, one who has the time and the intensity of interest to know his children and love them as they need to be loved. What a special loss to children of Christian parents, and to their fathers, also! What a loss to a young child's spirit when the earthly image of his Heavenly Father appears to be often indifferent and detached from the child's life!

For much of history, children of at least seven years of age or older worked alongside their parents in or around the home. Daily life was the context for continual teaching, nurturing, and parenting of children by their fathers, as well as their mothers. The industrial economy has not only shifted the location of work away from the home but it has demanded that men value their jobs ahead of their children. In the battle for a man's intensity of interest, career is expected to win, hands down.

New Approaches to a New Balance

Women who are sequencing and men who are demanding paternity leave when their children are born are two indications that long-standing approaches to balancing work and parenting are now being questioned. At the same time, some new approaches that attempt to speak to the concerns of both men and women are beginning to appear. Some parents find these approaches strike a more satisfactory balance of career and children.

Proverbs 31 offers women an alternative to the choice of either career or children. More and more women, not all motivated by specifically Christian concerns, are following it.

A mother of two young children in Miami is also a practicing attorney. Before her children were born, she was an assistant district attorney. When her children came, she changed the nature of her practice so that it could be done out of her home on a flexible schedule. Much of her work can be done using a small computer in the den. She is not a highly paid partner in a prestigious law firm but her practice is fulfilling and profitable while allowing her to care for her own children.

In New York a mother of two preschool children operates a small direct sales business out of her home. She is a sales and distribution representative for a line of inspirational Christian books and records. She can set her own schedule and do much of the work on evenings or weekends when her husband can help with child care.

Across the country countless other couples are experimenting with this Proverbs 31 model. These women entrepreneurs are among the fastest growing group of new entrepreneurs in the country.[8] They work hard but tailor their work schedules to meet the needs of their children. They have struck a balance that allows them to care for their children and still be successful designers, writers, word processors, salespersons, and paralegals, to name a few.[9]

There are probably as many ways to balance the demands of work and the needs of children as there are couples. One couple has some flexibility because the man owns his own construction company. He works a four-day, forty-hour week from Monday to Thursday (an option some companies are now making available to employees). He is home parenting his children on Friday and Saturday while his wife pursues her part-time career as a graphic artist.

Factory workers and women in clerical positions may not have such flexibility, but sometimes asking an employer begins to open up the possibility. Professionals have it somewhat easier. One couple I know, a dentist and a nurse, are able to control their own schedules enough to provide almost all the care of their young children.

Up to this point the options we have seen involve one spouse (usually the man) having a full-time career and the other (usually the woman) having a part-time one. In all these cases, the woman involved was not displeased with that choice. She wanted to have a career, but also to care for her children.

What happens if both spouses feel called to full-time careers? The choice seems to be "occasional parenting" for their children, or perhaps one spouse (the woman) working full time for a few years while the other (the man) assumes child-care responsibilities. After an agreed on period of time, they alternate.

These are compromises at best, with all the drawbacks of compromises. A more radical and perhaps more equitable and satisfying approach is being lived out by a couple in Pittsburgh. They call their approach "coparenting and coworking."

Mutuality, Work, and Parenting

Gail and Ken Heffner have three preschool children and two part-time jobs. It did not just happen (the part-time jobs); they intended it to be that way.

Ken and Gail believe that one effective way to balance the demands of careers and caring for their children is for both parents to have "permanent part-time work." In this way both parents are able to exercise their gifts in the world of work as, they believe, God intended. Each is also free to share fully in parenting their children.

For the Heffners, it is important that they both work and both are equal coparents of their children because the command given by God in Genesis 1:28 was given to both Adam and Eve. God said they were to "be fruitful and multiply" (to be parents) and to "subdue the earth" (to work).

If, however, either spouse is forced to choose either work or parenting, something valuable is lost. Fathers lose the privilege of nurturing their children. Society loses the contribution of a woman's talents in the marketplace. Children lose the richness of nurture offered by both parents.

The Heffners often use the term mutuality to describe what they are trying to do. Mutuality is a full and equal sharing in all the tasks and responsibilities, joys, and privileges of working and parenting. It especially applies to chores around the house; for example, Ken does his share of the grocery shopping.

He tells of an incident that illustrates how strange this mutuality appears to some people. He was out doing the grocery shopping one day with the children. A woman pushing her cart next to his looked at the children, smiled, and commented that he must be babysitting. "No," he replied. "I'm not babysitting. I'm their father."

No one would think a mother who was caring for her own children was babysitting. Parents do not babysit their own children. But it is still strange to see fathers so involved in child care, especially of young children.

Obviously, this coparenting aspect of their mutuality does not fit easily into the mold of one full-time breadwinner and one full-time parent. And the Heffners feel that when two parents each have full-time careers and send their children to day care, the result is usually no parenting. Their answer is permanent part-time work.

Both Gail and Ken work at part-time jobs that consume fifteen to twenty-five hours per week. They intend to continue that at least until their children are all in college. Ken is the director of college activities for a small nearby college. Gail works approximately fifteen hours per week as an organizational development specialist with a company that offers technical assistance to nonprofit organizations.

Permanent part-time work means for them just what it says: They will accept only part-time work. In that way they feel they can strike the right balance of career and caring for their children.

Within the context of mutuality of work and children, flexibility is another rule they live by. Being flexible means each spouse carries out those family responsibilities (such as shopping or balancing the checkbook) that he or she does best. Flexibility means encouraging other couples to feel free to choose if one spouse should work outside the home and one inside (or not at all) and then switching these roles every few years. That way the children can be nurtured by both parents. Their advice is to work out what seems best for you within the context of mutuality and then keep flexible as you juggle schedules and make sacrifices to make it work.

There are variations on this concept of permanent part-time work, and its advocates are growing. For instance, Benjamin Spock suggests that one alternative to day care is for "one or both parents to cut down to less than full time jobs for 2–3 years" until the children can go nursery school or a day-care center.[10]

Job sharing is also beginning to emerge as another variation. Commonly it consists of one job shared roughly equally by two people (usually women). Some employers are also offering flexible work schedules that allow for special child-care needs. Nevertheless, even these approaches to balancing work and children can be frustrating.

Ken Heffner shared one of his frustrations. He works at his particular job because it is so hard to practice what he considers his real vocation on a part-time basis: "I feel my calling vocationally is to be a journalist. But I'm not as good a journalist as I could be because I can't give it enough time right now." Ken does not regret his choice to be a coparent to his children but he recognizes the sacrifices and frustrations that result.

Frustration over slowed career development is one of those experienced by parents who pull back on job time to spend more time with their children. Part-time work usually pays no fringe benefits and results in slower and fewer promotions and raises. Parents who commit to it will have to face their fears of losing those promotions and the status that goes with them.

These frustrations and fears are inherent in "the fundamental conflict between the imperatives of career and parenting" or, to put it another way, in the conflict "between achievement on the world's terms and on one's own."[11] "Real men" (and women) work full time and make success their goal. Real parents make raising well-adjusted physically, emotionally, and spiritually whole children their goal.

New Attitudes

All around the country, couples are struggling to recover a healthy balance of the demands of career and children in their lives. Their goal is the congenial blending of work and family into a single, integrated career. A worthy goal, this promises to help recover much of the nurture that children are losing today. Achieving it throughout society, however, will require a new set of attitudes toward work itself, sex roles, and child rearing.

The male variety of individualism (which we have called careerism to distinguish it from the female variety, feminism) is built on certain attitudes and assumptions about the nature of a job. Because men have been in the full-time work world longer and more completely than women, men have tended to absorb these attitudes more fully. These attitudes, as they relate to children and families, may be summarized this way: Work schedules are more important than family schedules and work takes precedence over family. [12]

On the basis of these attitudes and the values embedded in them, many men feel justified (if not compelled) to accept work schedules that result in their neglect of family. They feel helpless to resist (or happy to accede to) company expectations that they will move their families every two to three years to get a promotion, regardless of the feelings of spouse or children. These men know they will receive little more than scorn if they should want to stay home with a sick child or ask for paternity leave to care for a newborn.

A generation of feminism has sold these same attitudes and tendencies to many women also. From a beginning that stressed the need for women to be free to choose, now there seems "only one choice for any self-respecting, well-educated, interesting woman: to work outside the home." It is simply not "right" for an intelligent, capable woman to "waste" herself at home with children. For women, as well as for men, at work is the only place where "real work" is accomplished. [13] The same attitudes that trap men into putting their work before their family's needs are now trapping women.

Can this situation ever change? When Ken Heffner's boss called to recruit him for the position of director of college activities, Ken said he would interview only if the job were made part time. Within weeks, the job description was rewritten; Ken accepted.

Women are wrestling with the stress of bearing children and then having to go off and leave them in the care of others almost immediately. Some are dropping the two-ton briefcase altogether and sequencing. When they return to work, many will want— and demand—only part-time work.

Ellen is a young woman who is helping change attitudes and practices in the workplace just by her example. She left an important, influential job as book editor for the *Wall Street Journal* to be a full-time mother to her infant son.

Her colleagues could not understand why she would prefer to "exchange a larger world for a smaller one, greater responsibilities for ones more petty or limited," and influence over many people for control over just one.[14] After all, everyone knows that "bigger is better" and "the many are more important than the few." She must have been blinded by maternal instinct; she must not understand what she is doing, they thought.

But Ellen understood exactly what she was doing and why. Maybe she could not convince her colleagues, but when one of their best and brightest do something so radical, they ask why and listen to the answer. Attitudes can begin to change.

Ellen had been captured by a bigger, deeper truth than "bigger is better" or "the many are more important than the few."

Christianity teaches us that each soul is uniquely valuable because it has been loved into existence by God. The destiny of each soul is supremely important . . . . It is not a greater thing to sacrifice one's life for a nation of people rather than one person; in either case, the sacrifice is noble or even allowable because the mortal life of our immortal soul is being surrendered for the mortal life of another immortal soul.[15]

Ellen knew the sacrifice was worth it. She would be able to give her son more and to give it more intensely than she would be able to give her legion of readers in the *Wall Street Journal*. For her and her son, that was exactly the right choice.

Men and women such as Ken, Gail, and Ellen are helping to bring change to the marketplace. When fathers start to consider that caring for their children is as important as their careers, they will demand work schedules that permit them the time they need for their families. When the best available employees (who happen to be women) demand that employers respect and accommodate their commitments to parenting—through providing part-time jobs, job sharing, and regular, paid maternity leave—change will begin to creep across the work world.

When men and women routinely demand change, perhaps the workplace *can* be restructured. The vision may become reality. Both men and women will be able to choose to work and to be parents.

A staggering vision this, so revolutionary does it seem. Present attitudes toward work, its organization, and method of accomplishment would be replaced by "a new set of social arrangements in which work becomes itself another aspect of nurture, transcends its present character of self aggrandizement, and comes to serve the needs, not merely of the living but of generations to come."[16]

This vision encompasses much more than women's liberation. It involves a true liberation of both men and women from a stressful, fragmented, unbalanced lifestyle to one where work and parenting are integrated into one single "career." It offers a more relaxed, balanced, and healthy lifestyle where "much less importance is given to outside jobs and more to the activities of the close community and family."[17]

Men, women, and children all need the liberation such changes will bring. The woman attorney in Miami remembers well how she was accused of wasting a scarce law school position (and robbing a man of it) by deciding to stay home and work part time so she could care for her children. Some people may think of Ken Heffner as merely a Mr. Mom.

These attitudes are dangerous to the health and welfare not only of adults but of their children. Much of the nurture and care that children no longer receive from their parents or anyone will be restored when these attitudes change. Men and women must come to feel that caring for their own children at home is at least as important, fulfilling, and *socially significant* as any other activity. Then both male careerists and radical feminists will no longer be able to make men and women feel like apologizing for deciding to make caring for children their "main career."[18]

Men Growing Up

We men can look forward to some benefits from these changes, too! Harry Stein, writing about the high cost of being a good father, related how he began to experience the dramatic "power of the emotions associated with parenthood" when he took an active role in parenting his two young children.[19]

Harry faced a deadline. His column for a major national magazine had to be on the editor's desk in six hours. He knew it would be at least twenty-four hours late. The "blame" for this, he knew, belonged to his four-month-old son Charlie (who had not yet slept four hours straight) and Charlie's older sister. She had brought the flu bug home from nursery school and had spread it around the family.

Harry was a stay at home parent. His career as a writer permitted him that flexibility. His wife worked outside the home. He knew he was paying a price in professional productivity for his decision to care for his children, a price, he understood, his wife and countless other women had paid for years.

He struggled with regret in being further behind in his career (and, therefore, as others would see it, in life) than he had once expected to be by now. He felt he was expected to pursue the Nobel Prize in literature, but had chosen instead to slacken the pace of his career to devote time to his children. Regrets or not, he knew he had to do it.

Harry found that parenting his children was a case of "try it, you'll like it." He began to immerse himself in the lives of his two young children, and found that "what I have with my children is priceless beyond measure; those thousands of hours on the floor amidst blocks and puzzlepieces and assorted dollies . . . of concocting games and stories and songs and simply sitting around not doing much at all, have been the most gratifying, the most emotionally satisfying of my life."[20]

Harry Stein has grown up, as he put it. He had made a hard choice (slackened the pace) and followed through on it. He had chosen to restore the balance of his life in favor of his children because he knew it was the right thing to do. In doing what was right, Harry discovered how dramatically and how wonderfully children can infuse life with something special.

Women have known it all along. Children are not only a gift from God, but vessels of the grace of God to their parents. They are vessels of grace not only (or even primarily) because they smile at us and challenge us to love them even more than we think we are able, but because they do require sacrifices and the making of hard choices for the right reasons.

Challenging us to grow up in this way, children are used by God to shape their parents more fully into God's image. Perhaps children are a vessel of God's "common grace" to Christians and unbelievers alike. But Christian parents are offered the special opportunity by God to share with Him in creating and nurturing another human made in His image. This adds an almost sacramental aspect to Christian parenthood.[21]

For the last century, most of the grace that children offer parents has been channelled to women. Men simply have not been there to receive it. But those who are, like Harry Stein and Ken Heffner, have found the rewards of parenting are more than worth the sacrifices and demands.

Harry Stein's words are a challenge to all fathers, especially we who are Christians. Harry has his priorities straight.

> Absolutely, I'd like to be forging ahead professionally. But even now, at this moment, on the edge of nodding out, I am sustained by the certainty that my children are a pair of worthies in the making, that they will arrive at adulthood with consciences intact, that they will be capable of giving love as it has been given them.
>
> And though I never thought I'd say it, this I would not trade for an armful of Nobel Prizes.[22]

We Christian fathers surely cannot want any less for our children. God Himself has given them to us as "worthies in the making." Yet only to the extent to which we give them of ourselves, and only as we allow them to see God their Heavenly

Father through us, will they arrive at adulthood with consciences intact and capable of giving love to God as we have given it to them.

Being a Christian father (or mother, for that matter) is no small task. It demands priorities that recognize the eternal, life-shaping nature of that undertaking. It demands giving of ourselves to our children, sometimes giving even more than we think we have. But it remains true with parenting what Jesus said in another context long ago: "Give, and it will be given to you. A good measure, pressed down, shaken together and running over, will be poured into your lap. For with the measure you use, it will be measured to you."[23]

We parents know we can never outgive God. He gives us the most precious gifts through our children.

NINE

Hope for
Recovery of Childhood

Tony Campolo tells the story of the black preacher whose Easter sermon captures the spirit of Christian hope. It is Friday, the preacher moans, and Jesus is dying on the cross. Satan and his forces are throwing a party. Even the sky is dark. All hope is gone.

But then the old preacher's voice rises and he shouts with glee: "Yes, it's Friday, but Sunday's comin'!" Things looked hopeless on that first Good Friday but Sunday was coming. Jesus would rise and hope would rise with Him.[1]

We could look back over this survey of childhood and feel like those Christians on that first Good Friday. Although the situation seems hopeless, that is not the case at all. There are signs that childhood and all its benefits can be protected and preserved.

A Renewal of Concern for Childhood

The number of abortions has dropped recently, representing the first such decline since 1969. The abortion rate is still high (over 1 million per year) but any decline is a good sign. It is especially encouraging when coupled with the fact that the birth rate has begun to increase. Between 1980 and 1986, the number of children under five years old increased by 11 percent.[2]

This increased birth rate is being widely attributed to the fact that the post–World War II baby boomers, many of whom postponed parenthood to establish careers, are now beginning their families. Whatever the cause, more "wanted" children being born and fewer "unwanted" children being aborted are positive developments.

Recent surveys also point to a renewed appreciation by adults of the problems children face, and the importance of helping children be happy and emotionally secure, not just academic achievers. A recent poll of readers of *Parents* magazine revealed that what these parents want most for their children is that they be happy and satisfied with themselves. Academic or other achievements clearly took second place.[3]

A 1986 nationwide survey of parents was equally encouraging. It revealed that a vast majority of parents recognize that the problems facing children—poverty, abuse, suicide, and drugs—have mushroomed in recent years.

Less than half of the parents surveyed felt that most American children are basically happy or get a good education. A substantial majority said they would be willing to pay higher taxes to support drug prevention programs, better schools, and day-care programs.[4]

Pollster Lou Harris, who conducted the survey, summed up the results in this way.

> The American people have come to a new consciousness about children, that long forgotten minority in our midst. It's plain that the American people are ripe and ready for leadership to emerge that will call upon some sacrifice (in) behalf of children.[5]

This new consciousness about children is a hopeful sign, and there is some leadership in place right now speaking out on behalf of children. Dr. James Dobson's efforts on behalf of children and the family are nothing less than a national treasure.

But one person is not enough. Now that the American people seem ready to act, more leadership is needed to encourage and direct them. This renewal of concern for children presents a good opportunity to begin to recover childhood.

Rediscovery of the Priority of Parenting

An apparent rediscovery of the priority of parenting among many adults is equally encouraging. A University of Wisconsin study of over 700 parents showed that two-thirds "considered parenting as their major source of satisfaction in life, as compared with work, personal development and other achievements."[6]

Some of these parents may well have postponed parenthood in pursuit of their careers. Some may have enjoyed the fruits of success and considered having no children at all. But as a University of Colorado sociologist observed, "people are finding that you do not find your life's fulfillment in things."[7] So they turned to having children. When we do indeed allow our children to be channels of God's grace to us, we often find much of the fulfillment we seek. Parents are rediscovering that today.

Parents also are beginning to rediscover the value of caring for their own children. A 1987 poll done for *Family Circle* magazine indicated that 70 percent of those polled (including both men and women) believed it is better for children to be cared for at home by their mothers than in a day care situation.[8]

Some couples might wish to substitute "parent" for "mother" in their reply, of course. Admittedly, this was probably a conservative group. Nonetheless, this poll indicates an encouraging openness among parents to balance their children's care needs versus their own career demands.

We have already met some of the men and women who are modeling lifestyles that integrate parenting with careers. Unfortunately, they are still too few and too isolated. If it is true that there is strength in numbers, they cannot feel strong. Some, especially those who are Christians, feel quite alone.

That was the experience of one Christian couple who decided that the wife would stay at home to care for their young children rather than work outside the home. The financial and lifestyle limitations this decision required were not their biggest problem, the husband said. "The real difficulty is the loneliness.

Our commitment to having one parent at home finds little support in the Christian community."[9]

This couple does not want any medals for doing what they felt was right. They do not want anyone to feel that they are right and others are wrong. What they missed from their church fellowship and friends was any indication that full-time parenting by the mother was worthwhile. In contrast, all the signals they received seemed to be aimed at convincing them that their choice was "at best, odd."[10]

This woman's model is not the industrious, mother-entrepreneur of Proverbs 31, but the more quiet mother of Titus 2. There, older women are told to teach their younger counterparts to stay at home and take care of their families.[11]

Certainly, this Titus 2 woman presents one more valid biblical model for women to choose. It is hardly less honorable (though surely less fashionable) than the more modern choice of full-time work outside the home. In view of the sacrifices it requires, this model may well be considered *more* honorable, *more* worthwhile.

Real freedom for women and true care for children means encouraging *all* of these options we have examined. Until the pendulum swings back to a more balanced view that recognizes the value of full-time parenting (by fathers, too), churches will need to preach those values *at least* as forcefully as those of equal opportunity for parents who choose full-time careers.

There is more that churches can do besides just preach on behalf of full-time parenting, however. Churches with day-care centers for working parents could offer a day of free care each week to stay at home parents. Seminars for Christian women that focus on how to manage both a home and a career could be balanced by seminars for men and women on how families can (and why they should) pull out of the rat race and live on less to give more to their children.[12]

Full-time motherhood (indeed, full-time parenthood) freely chosen out of love for one's children must surely be pleasing to God. Should not all Christians encourage it?

Reevaluation of Marriages and Commitment

In 1986 the U.S. Census Bureau reported that the divorce rate fell to its lowest level in over a decade.[13] The Bureau attributes this to a combination of two factors. Women are older at the time of their first marriage (having postponed marriage in favor of career) and marriages that occur later tend to be more stable and lasting.

But there also seems to be "a change in social attitudes toward maintaining marriages," a Bureau spokesperson said. In contrast to a period when divorce was the easiest answer, "Now, there is more of a feeling that people should try harder, should work more at it. Marriage is important. . . ."[14]

A representative of the country's largest video dating service summed up the attitude change. "Caution and commitment are in. Drinking, casual affairs and dead-end relationships are out."[15]

Fear of AIDS probably has something to do with this change in attitude toward commitment and marriage. But the change is also the sad result of experience; the deepest, most fulfilling relationships are only formed within lasting commitments. They take work to maintain, but they pay rich rewards, both for the marriage partners and for their children.

This social reevaluation of marriage represents a significant "window of opportunity" for Christians. We have traditionally held a high view of marriage and commitment that protected women and provided children the stable environment they need for emotional and spiritual health. Easy no-fault divorce has, by contrast, been a disaster for both women and children.[16] By strengthening our own marriages, we can offer society a powerful model of a rich relationship for which it hungers. This is a time of real opportunity.

Return to Sexual Sanity

In June 1987, a twelve-year-old San Francisco area boy sexually assaulted a four-year-old girl. The attack came two weeks after he spent over two hours on the telephone listening to accounts of rape and incest on a dial-a-porn service. His parents went to court to shut that service down.

They did not convince the judge to shut it down but, as a result of the incident, the California Public Utility Commission ordered the phone company to honor customers' requests to block all such calls from their phones. Similar rulings have been issued in Georgia, Pennsylvania, and other states. Bills to ban dial-a-porn services altogether are also pending in Congress. [17]

Pornography is under attack today, and for the first time in decades there is hope that its destructive influence can be greatly curtailed. Parents are saying "Enough!" to the sexual license threatening their children.

The National Coalition Against Pornography, led by Cincinnati pastor Dr. Jerry Kirk, has united a wide range of religious leaders to fight pornography. Dr. James Dobson, who served on the Attorney General's Commission on Pornography, has plunged wholeheartedly into the battle. His optimistic assessment of the outcome of the struggle is indicated by the title of his antipornography film, *The Winnable War.*

The Reagan administration's offensive against pornography was embodied in the Child Protection and Obscenity Act of 1987. Among other effects, the bill would make it illegal to produce, buy, or sell child pornography. It would also outlaw dial-a-porn services and allow government wiretaps in investigating allegations of the production and distribution of obscenity. [18]

This bill, and any similar or subsequent efforts, faces stiff opposition from the strong and profitable pornography industry itself as well as from misguided opponents crying "Censorship!" But seen together, these efforts justify the first real hope in over a generation that the scourge of pornography—especially child pornography—can be curtailed. A good beginning has been made, but it will require a long, hard struggle to lay to rest this scourge on our society and our children.

Fighting pornography is only a small first step in the process of restoring sexual sanity and respect for healthy sexual attitudes in our society. The terrible individual and social costs of widespread teenage pregnancy, for example, will not likely be reduced until the sexual enticements and inducements that permeate so much advertising, television, movies, and popular music are also reduced.

Joan Beck, a columnist for the *Chicago Tribune*, understands what needs to be done to protect young adolescents from the consequences of our sex-obsessed society. She called for greatly reducing the amount of sexual inducements that bombard our children and teenagers every day from all forms of popular media.[19]

It is time, Ms. Beck said, for adults to say, "Enough is enough!" and call a halt to the public obsession with sex as a "be-all, end-all and sell-all." Then, adults could begin to create an atmosphere in which children would learn healthy sexual values and teens could have the support they need to practice them. But, Ms. Beck asserts,

> . . . a big majority of adults would have to be good role models for sex-reserved-for-marriage-only. They would have to teach adolescents openly and convincingly why abstinence is worthwhile and demonstrate it in their own lives. They would have to say "no" before they could expect adolescents to do so. And they would also have to supervise teenage behavior more closely.[20]

Those are challenging words to our sex-obsessed society. But many thoughtful adults, like Ms. Beck, are calling for a return to sexual sanity, if only for the sake of our children. What an opportunity for Christians to join, and even lead, in re-creating an atmosphere where children and adolescents have an opportunity to learn and practice the tried and true wisdom of biblical, sexual values!

Reexamination of Public Attitudes Toward the Family

Signs of a new sensitivity to the needs of parents and children are emerging in the policies and practices of both business and governmental agencies. This reexamination of long-standing attitudes toward family concerns is cause for some hope that more significant changes are possible.

It is true, for example, that only about 6 percent of Americans work for companies that provide any kind of child-care assistance, but that is still an increase of nearly 50 percent since 1984. In the last decade the increase in the number of firm-sponsored and paid child-care programs is over 2000 percent![21]

In Boston the Stride-Rite Corporation, longtime manufacturer of children's shoes, provides low-cost child care for its employees at their worksite. An insurance company in Fort Wayne, Indiana, has a flexible hours policy that allows employees to adjust work schedules to care for their own children.[22]

Maternity leave is also beginning to gain some acceptance. Studies show that young children benefit from the full-time care of at least one parent during their early months of life.[23] More and more working parents—fathers as well as mothers—are seeking the freedom to spend this special time of bonding with their newborn without losing their jobs. Procter and Gamble, one of the nations' largest companies, provides mothers with six months maternity leave (unpaid) and allows workers to exchange vacation days for child-care allowance.

A 1988 Labor Department report states that as many as 50 percent of the nation's employers have instituted such practices as flexible hours, flexible leave policies (where vacation days can be used for child care), and job sharing.[24] These are modest beginnings, but they do help working parents care for their own children.

These policies were largely forced on employers by the influx of women into the workforce, a trend not likely to be reversed any time soon. As women rise to higher positions and as companies become more and more dependent on women workers, businesses will see that their best interests include accommodation of the child-care needs and desires of their women employees (and men employees also). The alternative will be to lose their best workers to companies who do.

Government bodies are also beginning to respond to pressure from working parents. In early 1988 the Internal Revenue Service opened a dozen on-site child-care centers for its nation-wide workforce of over 100,000. The weekly price of $60 to $90 is relatively modest. Nine states currently have laws that require employers to guarantee women four months of maternity leave and reinstatement to their jobs upon return. The U.S. Supreme Court has upheld a challenge to California's maternity leave law, holding that such special treatment of pregnant workers did not constitute illegal discrimination.

The introduction into Congress in early 1987 of the Family and Medical Leave Act is another hopeful sign for parents and children. This bill would require firms with fifteen or more employees to permit *both* mothers and fathers up to eighteen weeks of unpaid, job-guaranteed leave to care for a newborn baby, a newly adopted child, or one who is sick. Up to twenty-six weeks of job-protected unpaid leave would be provided in cases of worker illness or pregnancy.

One of the bill's most exciting aspects is the provision for paternity leave. Currently no state laws provide for it. Men who wish for it still face even more opposition than women. But men are demanding it (that is why it is in the federal bill) and making *some* gains. In Pittsburgh the city schools now grant child-care leave on the same basis for both men and women.

Seen in perspective, these are all small steps forward but there is good reason to believe more will follow. Momentum is gathering in favor of the needs of families with young children. For example, President Reagan ordered that all newly proposed federal policies or regulations be accompanied by a family impact statement. He sees this as a means to insure that the impact on families of any new federal policies or regulations would be considered before they were adopted.

This family impact statement would evaluate policies and regulations on the basis of such criteria as whether they promote or undermine family stability and the marriage commitment, their effect on parental authority and rights, and their impact on family income and the message they send to young people.[25]

This initiative represents the administration's attempt to put the family right at the center of the public policy making process. There is still a long way to go to move the country into a true prochildren and profamily position where child bearing and child rearing are given the priority they deserve, but the family impact statement requirement and the introduction of The Family and Medical Leave Act are encouraging signs indeed.

Some significant challenges remain, however. The current day-care situation presents too many risks to too many young, vulnerable children. As T. Berry Brazelton observes, "We can't afford to have half our future citizens, children under five, placed in second rate care-giving situations."[26] It is neither wise nor compassionate.

Even more frightening are the social consequences of the current two-tier day-care system. Such a system allows poor (often minority) children to be cared for in second- or third-rate situations while a limited supply of good quality day care is available only to affluent children. This is both unjust and unwise. It perpetuates rather than ameliorates class divisions and social handicaps. It promotes rather than eliminates a "permanent underclass" of minority children who start life with one more handicap.

Making a certain minimum quality and quantity of day care available nationally will be expensive, and there is no guarantee Americans are willing to pay the price. Federal and state funds supporting subsidized day care have been cut in recent years. As a result, fewer children than ever are in subsidized day care, yet more children than ever are eligible.[27]

Current welfare policies push poor, usually single mothers to go to work and to put their children in cheap, usually poor-quality day care. It might be of more benefit in the long run to help keep these mothers at home with their young children. One at-home welfare mother saw the wisdom in that: "I'm the only thing between my kid and the drug pusher on the street. As long as I'm here, my kids have got a chance."[28]

Certainly poor mothers have as much right to care for their own children at home as do middle- or upper-income mothers; and their children need them at least as much! These women need help to become self-supporting with at-home work or work during school hours.[29]

The federal government can give equal recognition to parents who stay at home to care for their children. Equal individual retirement account (I.R.A.) payments, social security deposits for at-home parents, and special loans and mortgages for such families would help restore the balance of recognition and appreciation between those parents who choose to work outside the home (often requiring day care) and those who choose to care for their own children at home.

The great unanswered question that remains is whether Americans are determined to make caring for children a priority again, and if so, if they are willing to pay the price for it. Marian Blum, author of *The Day Care Dilemma*, put the challenge this way:

> Children are entitled to a healthy, secure, consistent, loving, disciplined, warm, caring, nurtured, unpressured infancy and childhood. It is primarily the responsibility of parents to so provide. But, it is the responsibility of the greater society to create structures and policies that enable parents to do so. Society must re-think its priorities. If children are as important as offshore oil; if they are as interesting as computers; if they are as vital to the survival of the United States as nuclear missiles; if they are a national treasure equal to the Grand Canyon; then *someone will have to raise them*. And someone, including parents and the larger society, will have to pay for that care.[30]

There *are* reasons to be encouraged. But much progress remains to be made. All of us, parents of young children or not, must come to see how important it is to pay for that care children need.

Reawakening to Spiritual Values

The prophet Isaiah tells of a future golden age of peace when the Messiah shall reign, all creatures will live together in harmony, and "a little child will lead them."[31] One part of that prophecy has partially been fulfilled. Children are doing some leading today. They are leading their parents back to church.

As the baby boomers begin to have children, their attendance at church increases noticeably. A study by Hartford Seminary's Center for Social and Religious Research found about a 10 percent increase over the early 1970s in the number of people thirty-one to forty-two years old who attend religious services three times a month or more.[32]

Why this sudden turn to church by a once rebellious, religiously indifferent generation? The study's director put it this way: "As people move into the later stages of life, they're looking for more stable, more lasting kinds of values and they find the church supportive of that."[33]

A similar study by the Lutheran Church in America found that these new parents also were directly motivated to return to church out of concern for their children. "They want help in raising their children so that church will be a part of their lives, so that they will have good values and so that they will belong, through baptism, to God."[34]

Concern that their children have good values is by no means the worst motivation for coming to church! This development at least provides an opportunity to help turn many of the current generation of parents from an obsession with success and sex (or is it sex and success?) to the source of the real and enduring values they seek, Jesus Christ.

Churches have opportunity here, but there are also dangers. Good moral values are important, but they are no substitute for faith. Children and parents need a living faith in order to give good values meaning and endurance. Good values are more than another attribute of a successful child.

God will not be used that way. He is not simply a tool for

imparting good values to children. He is not some celestial kill-joy or parental policeman always saying no and punishing naughty boys and girls. As we welcome these parents into our churches, we must guard both them and their children against such a shrunken, trivialized picture of our sovereign God. Churches can offer these parents help in the moral formation of their children, but only in the context of "the authentic depth and challenge" of the historic Christian faith.[35]

What More Can We Do?

As some parents are modeling new approaches to parenting, some churches are accepting new ministry challenges on behalf of children and families. Their efforts, too, are good beginnings, and they show that much more remains to be done.

The church where I had an office for five years had a day-care center in one wing. This all too typical city church with a large building and an endowment had a small congregation. The space occupied by the day-care center would otherwise have been unused.

The church saw an opportunity for using that space for a much-needed ministry. Both the space and the utilities were donated. The center can charge moderate fees and still pay its staff above average salaries. The quality of care, and caring, by that staff (which understands their work as *ministry*) is well above average.

A suburban church within a few miles of my office opened a ministry to neighborhood latch-key children. They started an after school program that included snacks, recreation, creative Bible teaching, and time for homework. It was a big undertaking and attendance was small at first, but it was also an important ministry to those children and their families.

Single mothers represent a largely untapped ministry. Single moms need friends (single friends without children or parents in two-parent families) who can take their children once in a while so Mom can go out! Even the most dedicated single parent needs a break now and then!

Children of single parents also offer real ministry opportunities. Usually it is the father who is absent. These children need interaction with a mature, caring adult male who will show them what "maleness" is all about. Boys need this for obvious reasons. Girls need it in order to relate well to men as adults (especially in marriages).

The national Big Brother and Big Sister organizations have been attempting something like this for years. But children need more than just adult friends. They need adults who love them, love Jesus Christ, and show what that looks like in everyday life. Children cannot get that from just anyone. It is an exciting ministry opportunity, especially for single young adults or married couples (with or without children).

The divorce epidemic has not spared our churches. It has underscored once again the absolute necessity of helping people build and maintain strong marriages, and supporting them through the hard work and pain required. Sermons, ceremonies, celebrations, classes, and an atmosphere within the congregation that encourages people to work at their marriages and to "hang in there" during the tough times because "we're with you" are all positive steps in recovering some of the benefits of lasting marriages so often lost to children today.

Churches can offer parents the help they need to keep things in perspective. Equality is important, work and success are proper in their place, but children are a gift from the Lord. Surely caring for them for a decade or decade and a half is at least as worthy as any other undertaking. Church fellowships can offer parents the support and encouragement they need to be full-time parents and proud (not guilty) of it.

Choosing to swim upstream against the prevailing currents of individualism and careerism (that even go unchallenged in many churches) does not require legislating that everyone else make the same choice. But we ought to at least feel equally worthy with those who choose differently. And living out such a choice will, for the near future at least, require courage and support. It is, after all, different, and being different is always risky.

Where will this courage to be different come from? Where will those who make choices in favor of their children, choices that reject prevailing attitudes, find support? There is only one source: from within a group of people who have always had to risk being different, who always had to try to live in tension with the society around them. They are known as Christians.

It is called being in the world, but not of it, living our daily lives in the same environment as everyone else but being willing at the same time to hold the values of that environment up to critical scrutiny.[36] It means marching, when necessary, to a different drummer. This is the kind of people children need today.

Christians are called to be like little children [37] and one thing both Christians and children have in common is hope. We live in an encouraging time; all is not lost for children. These signs we have noted offer reason for hope that much of the vanishing treasure of childhood can still be recovered.

For many children this is not a happy time. But God's Spirit *is* at work. He *will* accomplish His purposes, and He does not need our help. In the meantime, however, God's "little children" surely do.

Source Notes

Introduction

1. Neil Postman, *The Disappearance of Childhood* (New York: Dell, 1982), p. 99.
2. Cynthia Painter, "We Want Happy Kids, Not Whizzes," *USA Today*, February 18, 1987: p. 22.
3. Christine Davidson, *Staying Home Instead: How to Quit the Working-Mom Rat Race and Survive Financially* (Lexington, MA: Lexington Books, 1986), p. 139.
4. Davidson, *Staying Home*, p. 28.
5. David E. Anderson, "Church's Atmosphere is the Main Concern of Baby Boomers," *Washington Post*, January 31, 1986.
6. Davidson, *Staying Home*, p. 17.
7. *See* Proverbs 31:28.
8. Postman, *Disappearance*, p. 11.

Chapter 1

1. Phillippe Aries, *Centuries of Childhood, A Social History of Family Life* (New York: Random House, 1962), p. 128.
2. Ibid., p. 50.
3. Neil Postman, *The Disappearance of Childhood* (New York: Dell, 1982), pp. 13–15.
4. Matthew 19:13–15.
5. Matthew 18:1–5, KJV. Jesus warns His questioners to become like little children if they would enter heaven.
6. "Lee Iaccoca Is Down on Yuppies," *USA Today*, February 11, 1986, p. 20.
7. Psalm 127:3, NAS.
8. Alvin Toffler, *Future Shock* (New York: Random House, 1970), pp. 10–11.

9. Christopher Lasch, *Haven in a Heartless World* (New York: Basic Books, 1977), p. 8.

10. Matthew 19:6, KJV.

11. Brigitte Berger and Peter L. Berger, *The War Over the Family* (Garden City, NY: Doubleday, 1983), p. 37.

12. Ross T. Bender, *Christians in Families* (Scottdale, PA: Herald Press, 1982), p. 85.

13. Quoted in Rodney Clapp, "Vanishing Childhood, Part 2," *Christianity Today* (June 15, 1984), p. 18.

14. Robert Bellah et al., *Habits of the Heart: Individualism and Commitment in America* (New York: Harper & Row, 1985), p. 3.

15. Ibid., p. 5.

16. Ibid., p. 6.

17. *The Family: Preserving America's Future*, The Report of the White House Working Group on the Family, November, 1986, p. 13.

18. Bender, *Christians in Families*, p. 85.

19. Research conducted at Bowling Green State University, Bowling Green, Ohio, and cited in Michelle Healy, "The Downside of Raising a Family," *USA Today*, Oct. 9, 1986, p. B1.

20. Marie Winn, *Children Without Childhood* (New York: Penguin Books, 1984), p. 5.

21. David Elkind, *The Hurried Child* (Reading, MA: Addison-Wesley, 1981), p. 197.

22. Ibid., pp. 192–196.

23. Working Group on the Family, p. 24.

24. Working Group on the Family, p. 25.

25. Colleen O'Conner, "Affluent America's Forgotten Children," in *Newsweek* (June 2, 1986), p. 21.

26. Jane Blotzer, "The Feminization of Poverty," *Pittsburgh Post-Gazette*, Oct. 13, 1986, p. 9.

27. Working Group on the Family, p. 26.

28. Colleen O'Conner, "Affluent America's," p. 21.

29. Ibid.

30. Jim Gallagher, "The Children Are Suffering," *Pittsburgh Post-Gazette*, October 13, 1986, p. 10.

31. Sirgay Sanges and John Kelly, "How to Be a Better (Working) Mother," *Redbook* (March, 1987), p. 94.

32. Lasch, *Haven*, p. xvi.

33. Bender, *Christians in Families*, p. 80.

34. Working Group on the Family, p. 14.

35. Matthew 19:14, NIV.

Chapter 2

1. Marie Winn, *Children Without Childhood* (New York, Penguin Books, 1981), p. 81.

2. Bruno Bettleheim, "The Importance of Play," *The Atlantic Monthly* (March, 1987), pp. 35–36.

3. T. Berry Brazelton, *Working and Caring* (Reading, MA: Addison-Wesley, 1987), p. 122.

4. Jeanette Gallagher and Judith Coche, "Hothousing: The Clinical and Educational Concerns Over Pressuring Young Children," *Early Childhood Research Quarterly* 2, no. 3 (September, 1987), pp. 207–208.

5. Ibid. *See also* James Dobson, *Dr. Dobson Answers Your Questions* (Wheaton, IL: Tyndale House, 1982), pp. 78–79.

6. David Elkind, *The Hurried Child* (Reading, MA: Addison-Wesley, 1981), p. 31.

7. Bettleheim, *Play*, p. 37.

8. Quoted in Rodney Clapp, "Vanishing Childhood, Part 2," *Christianity Today* (June 15, 1984), p. 23.

9. Elkind, *Hurried Child*, p. 160.

10. "Drug Users Started at 12, Survey Shows," and "Under 15 Suicide Rate Up Sharply," *Pittsburgh Press*, September 18, 1986, p. A10.

11. Romans 6:23, NIV.

12. Elkind, *Hurried Child*, p. 121.

13. Brazelton, *Working*, pp. 122, 129.

14. Irving E. Sigel, "Does Hothousing Rob Children of Their Childhood?" *Early Childhood Research Quarterly* 2, no. 3 (September, 1987), p. 126.

15. Lawrence J. Schweinhart, David P. Weikart, and Mary P. Larner, "Consequences of Three Pre-School Curriculum Models Through Age 15," *Early Childhood Research Quarterly* 1, no. 1 (March, 1986), p. 34–37. For a critique of that research and interpretation and the author's rejoinder, see *Early Childhood Research Quarterly* 1, no. 3 (September, 1986), p. 289–311.

16. Tynette W. Hills, "Children in the Fast Lane: Implications for Early Childhood Policy and Practice," *Early Childhood Research Quarterly* 2, no. 3 (September, 1987), p. 267.

17. Brazelton, *Working*, p. 129.

18. Winn, *Children*, p. 81.

19. Dolores Curran, *Stress and the Healthy Family* (Minneapolis, MN: Winston Press, 1985), p. 103.

20. Phillippe Aries, *Centuries of Childhood, A Social History of Family Life* (New York: Random House, 1962), p. 110.

21. Elkind, *Hurried Child*, p. 3.

22. Winn, *Children*, p. 42.

23. Interview with Robert Coles, "The Best Parents Learn From Their Children," *USA Today*, May 5, 1986, p. A13.

24. Winn, *Children*, p. 15.

25. Elkind, *Hurried Child*, p. 151.

26. Neil Postman, *The Disappearance of Childhood* (New York: Dell, 1982), p. 93.

27. Ibid.

28. Aries, *Centuries*, p. 50.

29. Jeannie Echenique, "Early Dating May Lead to Early Sex," *USA Today*, November 12, 1986, p. B1.

30. Elkind, *Hurried Child*, pp. 81–83.

31. Ibid. *See also* Curran, *Stress*, p. 103.

32. Philippians 4:8, NIV.

33. Romans 8:28, NAS.

34. Winn, *Children*, p. 54.
35. Postman, *Disappearance*, p. 97.

Chapter 3

1. Phillippe Aries, *Centuries of Childhood, A Social History of Family Life* (New York: Random House, 1962), p. 119.
2. Neil Postman, *The Disappearance of Childhood* (New York: Dell, 1982), p. 9.
3. "Sex and Schools," *Time* (November 24, 1986), p. 54.
4. Marie Winn, *Children Without Childhood* (New York: Penguin Books, 1984), pp. 73–74.
5. Ibid., p. 85.
6. *See* the excellent and comprehensive explanation of this in Postman, *Disappearance*, (New York: Dell, 1982).
7. Nancy Olin, quoted in "Sex and Schools," *Time* (November 24, 1986), p. 60.
8. Robert Bianco, "TV Shows Enjoy New Sexual Freedom as Networks Loosen Bonds," *Pittsburgh Press*, January 5, 1987, p. D4.
9. Postman, *Disappearance*, p. 79.
10. Bianco, "TV Shows," p. D4.
11. Ibid.
12. Aries, *Centuries*, p. 100.
13. Winn, *Children*, p. 71.
14. Alfie Kohn, "Shattered Innocence," *Psychology Today* (February, 1987), p. 54.
15. Ephesians 5:21–33, NIV.
16. Aries, *Centuries*, p. 103.
17. Richard E. McLawhorn, "Summary of the Final Report of the Attorney General's Commission on Pornography," Cincinnati, OH: National Coalition Against Pornography, 1986, p. 10.
18. *Time*, p. 63.
19. Joan Beck, "Teen Sex Presents an Adult Dilemma," *Pittsburgh Press*, December 19, 1986, p. C3.

20. Josh McDowell, "The Gap Widens," *Eternity* (June, 1987), p. 15.
21. *See* for example, *Psychology Today* (June, 1986), p. 10.
22. Quoted in David Elkind, *The Hurried Child* (Reading, MA: Addison-Wesley, 1981), p. 60.
23. Ibid., p. 57.

Chapter 4

1. Josh McDowell, "The Gap Widens," *Eternity* (June, 1987), p. 15.
2. Brigitte Berger and Peter L. Berger, *The War Over the Family* (Garden City, NY: Doubleday, 1983), p. 60.
3. P. D. Eastman, *Are You My Mother?* (New York: Random House, 1960).
4. Neil Gilbert, "The Unfinished Business of Welfare Reform," *Society* (March–April, 1987), p. 5.
5. Ibid.
6. David Elkind, *The Hurried Child* (Reading, MA: Addison-Wesley, 1981), p. 152.
7. Benjamin Spock and Michael B. Rothenberg, *Dr. Spock's Baby and Child Care* (New York: Pocket Books, 1985), pp. 672–73.
8. *The Family: Preserving America's Future*: The Report of the White House Working Group on the Family, November, 1986, pp. 24–25.
9. James Q. Wilson and Richard J. Herrnstein, *Crime and Human Nature* (New York: Simon and Schuster, 1985).
10. White House Working Group, pp. 24–25.
11. Spock and Rothenberg, *Baby and Child Care*, pp. 668–69.
12. Ibid., pp. 664–65.
13. Armand M. Nicholi, Jr., "Commitment to Family," in *Family Building: Six Qualities of a Strong Family*, ed. George Rekers (Ventura, CA: Regal Books, 1985), p. 53.
14. *See* Berger and Berger, *War*, p. 153, and also Erik Erikson, *Children and Society* (New York: Norton, 1950).

15. Judson J. Swihart and Steven L. Brigham, *Helping Children of Divorce* (Downers Grove, IL: InterVarsity Press, 1982), p. 35.
16. Archibald D. Hart, *Children and Divorce: What to Expect, How to Help* (Waco, TX: Word Books, 1982), p. 28.
17. Elkind, *Hurried Child*, p. 166.
18. Swihart and Brigham, *Children of Divorce*, p. 37.
19. White House Working Group, p. 26.
20. Ibid., p. 30.
21. Swihart and Brigham, *Children of Divorce*, p. 10.
22. Hart, *Children and Divorce*, p. 28.
23. "Divorce: Do It for the Kids," *Psychology Today* (July, 1987), p. 21. Cited is a study by Nicholas Long and Rex Forehand, *Journal of Abnormal Child Psychology* 15:15–28.
24. Hart, *Children and Divorce*, p. 28.
25. "Divorce," *Psychology Today*, p. 21.
26. Swihart and Brigham, *Children of Divorce*, p. 28.
27. Hart, *Children and Divorce*, p. 33.
28. Swihart and Brigham, *Children of Divorce*, p. 28.
29. Ibid., p. 34.
30. Erik Erikson, *Young Man Luther* (New York: W. W. Norton, 1958), pp. 122–23.
31. Oliver Chadwick, *The Reformation* (New York: Penguin Books, 1964), p. 45.
32. Ibid.
33. Erikson, *Luther*, p. 145.
34. Romans 1:17, KJV.
35. Erikson, *Luther*, p. 222.
36. Swihart and Brigham, *Children of Divorce*, p. 118.
37. "Divorce," *Psychology Today*, p. 21.
38. Matthew 18:6, NIV.

Chapter 5

1. Neil Gilbert, "The Unfinished Business of Welfare Reform," *Society* (March–April, 1987), p. 5.

2. Claudia Wallis, "The Child Care Dilemma," *Time* (June 22, 1987), p. 63.

3. T. Berry Brazelton, *Working and Caring* (Reading, MA: Addison-Wesley, 1987), p. 81.

4. Quoted in Robert J. Trotter, "Project Day Care," *Psychology Today* (December 1987), p. 36.

5. Ibid., p. 32.

6. T. Berry Brazelton provides a brief but helpful set of criteria for evaluating different kinds of day care in *Working and Caring*, Ch. 8. *See also* the helpful evaluation given by Benjamin Spock and Michael B. Rothenberg, *Dr. Spock's Baby and Child Care* (New York: Pocket Books, 1985), pp. 48–52.

7. Trotter, "Day Care," p. 36.

8. Spock and Rothenberg, *Baby and Child Care*, pp. 44–45; *see also* John Bowlby, *Attachment and Loss*, Vol. II, (Separation) (New York: Basic Books, 1983).

9. Dr. David Elkind quoted in Michelle Healy, "Child Care Merry-Go-Round Confuses Kids," *USA Today*, November 14, 1986, p. B1.

10. Wallis, "Child Care," p. 55.

11. Trotter, "Day Care," p. 33.

12. Marty Greavett, Cosby S. Rogers, and Linda Thompson, "Child Care Decisions Among Female Head of Households With School Age Children," *Early Childhood Research Quarterly* 2, no. 1 (March, 1987), p. 75.

13. Ibid., p. 76.

14. Trotter, "Day Care," p. 36.

15. I recognize, of course, that many women went into the workforce to support the national defense effort during World War II. This represents an exception to the general understanding of a woman's role in society at that time, however. After the war when the exceptional circumstances were gone, so were most of those women from the workforce.

16. Wallis, "Child Care," p. 63.

17. Betty Holcomb, " 'Where's Mommy?' The Great Debate Over the Effects of Day Care," *New York* (April 13, 1987), p. 76.

18. Spock and Rothenberg, *Baby and Child Care*, pp. 43–52.

19. Holcomb, "Where's Mommy?" p. 73.

20. Sandy Parker, "Good Day Care Can Produce Good Results," *USA Today*, July 10, 1987, p. D1.

21. Ibid. *See also* Brazelton, *Working*, p. 115.

22. "After 10 Year Day Care Study, Psychologist Changes His Stance," *Focus on the Family* (August, 1987), p. 10.

23. Holcomb, "Where's Mommy?" p. 78.

24. Ibid.

25. Ibid.

26. Mark 12:31, NIV.

27. Quoted in Paul D. Meier and Frank B. Minirth, "Spending Time Together" in *Family Building*, ed. George Rekers (Ventura, CA: Regal Books, 1985), p. 82.

28. Eleanor Weisberger, "Full Time Moms Develop Special Ties," *USA Today*, May 7, 1987. *See also* Spock and Rothenberg, *Baby and Child Care*, p. 52.

29. Holcomb, "Where's Mommy?" p. 74.

30. Marian Wright Edelman, "We're Putting Our Future at Risk," *USA Today*, November 12, 1987, p. A8. Ms. Edelman is president of the Children's Defense Fund.

Chapter 6

1. Christopher Lasch, *Haven in a Heartless World* (New York: Basic Books, 1977), p. 39.

2. Ibid.

3. Michelle Healy, "The Downside to Raising a Family," *USA Today*, October 9, 1986, p. B1.

4. Ibid.

5. Neil Postman, *The Disappearance of Childhood* (New York: Dell, 1982), p. 138.

6. Karen S. Peterson, "None is Enough," *USA Today*, April 16, 1987, p. D4.
7. Postman, *Disappearance*, p. 151.
8. Dolores Curran, *Stress and the Healthy Family* (Minneapolis, MN: Winston Press, 1985), p. 81.
9. Statistics furnished by the National Right to Life Movement, 419 7th St., N.W., #402, Washington, D.C. 20004.
10. Educational consultant Berk Sterling quoted in Curran, *Stress*, p. 118.
11. Matthew 6:21, NIV.
12. Josh McDowell, "The Gap Widens," *Eternity* (June, 1987), p. 19.
13. Armand M. Nicholi, Jr., "Commitment to Family," in *Family Building: Six Qualities of a Strong Family*, ed. George Rekers (Ventura, CA: Regal Books, 1985), p. 52.
14. Ibid., p. 53.
15. Sylvia Nasar, "Do We Live as Well as We Used To?" *Fortune* (September 14, 1987), p. 32.
16. Ibid., p. 44.
17. Ibid., p. 32.
18. Cited in J. Allen Petersen, "Family Happiness is Homemade," 10, no. 2 (February, 1986).
19. Marie Winn, *Children Without Childhood* (New York: Penguin Books, 1984), pp. 22–27.
20. Ibid., p. 43.
21. Nancy P. Alexander, "School Age Child Care: Concerns and Challenges," *Young Children* (November, 1986), p. 3.
22. Virginia Painter, "2.1 M Kids Find House Empty," *USA Today*, February 10, 1987, p. D1.
23. Jane Gottlieb, "Locking Out Problems of USA Latch Key Kids," *USA Today*, October 29, 1987, p. D1.
24. Lynette Long, "On My Own: Self Care for Kids at Home Alone," *Ms.* (June, 1986), pp. 59–60.
25. Alexander, "School Age Child Care," p. 4.
26. "Project Home Safe Set up to Help out Latch-Key Kids," *Pittsburgh Press*, October 29, 1987, p. 1.

27. Ibid., (quoting Health Undersecretary Don Newman).
28. Quoted in Robert J. Trotter, "Project Day Care," *Psychology Today* (December, 1987), pp. 34–35.
29. Thomas J. Long, "Children Are Victims of Today's Priorities," *USA Today*, December 4, 1985, p. A10. Long is associate professor of education at the Catholic University of America, Washington, D.C.
30. Ibid.
31. *See* Job 31:15 and Psalm 22:9, NIV, for example.
32. Luci Shaw, "Yes to Shame and Glory," *Christianity Today* (December 12, 1986), p. 23.
33. T. J. Long, "Children Are Victims," p. A10.

Chapter 7

1. Robert Ringer, *Looking Out for Number One* (New York: Fawcett, 1977), p. 12.
2. Stephen D. Eyre, *Defeating the Dragons of the World* (Downers Grove, IL: InterVarsity Press, 1987), p. 62.
3. Nena O'Neill and George O'Neill, *Open Marriage* (New York: Avon Books, 1972), pp. 47, 69.
4. Robert Bellah et al., *Habits of the Heart: Individualism and Commitment in America* (New York: Harper & Row, 1985), p. 16.
5. Sociologist Talcott Parsons quoted in Brigitte Berger and Peter L. Berger, *The War Over the Family* (Garden City, NY: Doubleday, 1983), p. 13.
6. Berger and Berger, *War*, p. 13.
7. L. Valeska, "If All Else Fails, I'm Still a Mother," in *Building Feminist Theory* (New York: Longmans, 1981), p. 81.
8. *See* 1 Corinthians 13: 4, 5, NIV.
9. Bellah et al., *Habits*, p. 109.
10. Ibid., p. 93.
11. Betty Friedan, *It Changed My Life* (New York: Random House, 1976), p. 33.

12. Ibid., p. 20.
13. Taken from the Statement of Purpose of the National Organization for Women (NOW), quoted in Friedan, *Changed Life*, p. 87.
14. Friedan, *Changed Life*, p. 22.
15. Ibid., p. 64.
16. Mary Frances Winters, "The Executive Mom," *USA Today*, December 8, 1986, p. A12.
17. Wally Metts, Jr., "Home Grown Kids Need a Full Time Mom," *Christianity Today* (March 6, 1987), p. 12.
18. Benjamin Spock and Michael B. Rothenberg, *Dr. Spock's Baby and Child Care* (New York: Pocket Books, 1985), pp. 36–37.
19. Leah Yarrow, "Why They Work," *Parents* (June, 1986), p. 85.
20. Winters, "Executive Mom," p. A12.
21. Inger Rudberg, quoted in Ross T. Bender, *Christians in Families* (Scottsdale, PA: Herald Press, 1982), p. 86.
22. Valeska, "If All Else Fails," p. 83.
23. See remarks attributed to Shulasmith Firestone in Bender, *Christians in Families*, p. 80.
24. Berger and Berger, *War*, p. 15.
25. David Elkind, *The Hurried Child* (Reading, MA: Addison-Wesley, 1981), pp. 26–27.
26. Neil Postman, *The Disappearance of Childhood* (New York: Dell, 1982), p. 151.
27. Beryl Lieff Benderly, "The Case for Working Moms," *Psychology Today* (October, 1987), p. 6.
28. Dr. Burton White, quoted in *Focus on the Family* (February, 1987), p. 5.
29. Dianne Hales, "Are Working Moms Good Mothers?" *Redbook* (March, 1987), p. 95.
30. Ibid., p. 172.
31. Dr. James Dobson, quoted in *Focus on the Family* (February, 1987), pp. 4–5.
32. Ibid.

33. Ibid.
34. Ibid.
35. Ibid.
36. Hales, "Working Moms," p. 172.
37. *The Family: Preserving America's Future*: The Report of the White House Working Group on the Family, November, 1986, p. 56.
38. Shirley Weltz, quoted in Bender, *Christians in Families*, p. 30.
39. Hales, "Working Moms," p. 172.
40. Matthew 16:15, NIV.
41. Richard John Neuhaus, *The Naked Public Square: Religion and Democracy in America* (Grand Rapids, MI: Eerdmans, 1984).

Chapter 8

1. Christine Davidson, *Staying Home Instead: How to Quit the Working-Mom Rat Race and Survive Financially* (Lexington, MA: Lexington Books, 1986), p. 27.
2. Ibid., p. 25.
3. Recently this strategy has been rediscovered in books such as Arlene Rosen Cardozo, *Sequencing* (New York: Atheneum, 1986).
4. Ibid.
5. Davidson, *Staying Home*, p. 137.
6. Harry Stein, "A Man of Progeny: The High Cost of Being a Good Father," *Esquire* (April, 1985), p. 38.
7. Ibid.
8. Davidson, *Staying Home*, p. 15.
9. Ibid., p. 102.
10. Benjamin Spock and Michael B. Rothenberg, *Dr. Spock's Baby and Child Care* (New York: Pocket Books, 1985), p. 49.
11. Stein, "Man of Progeny," p. 37.

12. Christopher Lasch, *Haven in a Heartless World* (New York: Basic Books, 1977), pp. xv, xvii.

13. Davidson, *Staying Home*, p. 13.

14. Ellen Wilson Fielding, "Career Change," *Christianity Today* (December 11, 1987), p. 27.

15. Ibid.

16. Lasch, *Haven*, p. xvii.

17. Spock and Rothenberg, *Baby and Child Care*, p. 40.

18. Ibid., p. 41.

19. Stein, "Man of Progeny," p. 38.

20. Ibid., p. 37.

21. Fielding, "Career Change," p. 27.

22. Stein, "Man of Progeny," p. 38.

23. Luke 6:38, NIV.

Chapter 9

1. Tony Campolo, "Tomorrow Is Sunday," speech given to annual meeting of the Million Dollar Roundtable (June 23–30, 1983).

2. Jane Gottlieb, "Boomer Babies Swell the Ranks in Pre-Schools," *USA Today*, December 18, 1987, p. D1.

3. Cynthia Painter, "We Want Happy Kids, Not Whizzes," *USA Today*, February 18, 1987, p. D2.

4. "Poll Shows Adults Concern for Children," *Pittsburgh Press*, September 24, 1986, p. A1.

5. Ibid.

6. Dolores Curran, *Stress and the Healthy Family* (Minneapolis, MN: Winston Press, 1985), p. 99.

7. Elizabeth R. Moen quoted in Judy Keen, "Boomers Bring Back Families with Kids," *USA Today*, December 16, 1986, p. A1.

8. *See* Nanci Hellmich, "How to Keep Your Marriage a Happy One," *USA Today*, December 21, 1987, p. A1. The survey was reported in the January 12, 1987, issue of *Family Circle*.

9. Wally Metts, Jr., "Home Grown Kids Need a Full-Time Mom," *Christianity Today* (March 6, 1987), p. 12.
10. Ibid.
11. *See* Titus 2:3–5, NIV.
12. Metts, "Home Grown Kids," p. 12.
13. "Divorce Rate Called Lowest in Years," *Pittsburgh Press*, April 8, 1987, p. A17.
14. Ibid.
15. Karen Petersen, "Singles: Marriage in; Affairs, Drinking Out," *USA Today*, January 22, 1987, p. Al.
16. *The Family: Preserving America's Future*: The Report of the White House Working Group on the Family, November, 1986, pp. 23–26.
17. Richard Lacayo, "Reach Out and Touch Someone," *Time* (December 21, 1987), p. 58.
18. "Trying to Close Some Obscenity Law Loopholes," *Christianity Today* (December 11, 1987), p. 57.
19. Joan Beck, "Teen Sex Presents an Adult Dilemma," *Pittsburgh Press*, December 19, 1986, p. C3.
20. Ibid.
21. Mark Memmott, "Child Care Plans Take First Steps," *USA Today*, June 17, 1987, p. B1.
22. William Dunn, "Child Care Helps Career Moms, Firms," *USA Today*, February 10, 1987, p. Al.
23. See discussion of this issue in chapter 5.
24. "60% of Firms Give Working Parents Flexibility, Study Finds," *Pittsburgh Press*, January 15, 1988, p. A7.
25. "Monitoring Government's Impact on the Family," *Christianity Today* (October 16, 1987), p. 52.
26. T. Berry Brazelton, *Working and Caring* (Reading, MA: Addison-Wesley, 1987), p. 64.
27. Christine Davidson, *Staying Home Instead: How to Quit the Working-Mom Rat Race and Survive Financially* (Lexington, MA: Lexington Books, 1986), p. 123.
28. Ibid., p. 145.
29. Ibid.

30. Marian Blum, *The Day Care Dilemma* (Lexington, MA: D. C. Heath and Co., 1983), pp. 117–18, quoted in Davidson, *Staying Home*, p. 122.

31. *See* Isaiah 11:1–9, NIV.

32. Joseph Berger, "Baby Boomers Turning to Religion," *Pittsburgh Post-Gazette*, November 27, 1986 (New York Times News Service).

33. Ibid.

34. David E. Anderson, "Church's Atmosphere is the Main Concern of Baby Boomers," *Washington Post*, January 31, 1986.

35. I have relied here on the perceptive analysis of Rodney Clapp, "Bull Market in Religion," *Christianity Today* (April 3, 1987), p. 15.

36. *See* John 15:19; 17:11, 14, and 1 John 2:15, for example.

37. Matthew 18:2–5.